FRANCIS FRITH'S

COVENTRY - A HISTORY AND CELEBRATION

Happy 94th birthday,

with love,

Christopher & Susan

THE FRANCIS FRITH COLLECTION

www.francisfrith.com

COVENTRY
A HISTORY AND CELEBRATION OF THE CITY

DAVID McGRORY

Produced by The Francis Frith Collection

www.francisfrith.com

First published in the United Kingdom in 2004 by
The Francis Frith Collection®

Hardback Edition 2004 ISBN 1-90493-818-3
Paperback Edition 2011 ISBN 978-1-84589-623-2

Text and Design copyright © The Francis Frith Collection®
Photographs copyright © The Francis Frith Collection®

The Frith photographs and the Frith logo are reproduced under licence from Heritage Photographic Resources Ltd, the owners of the Frith archive and trademarks

All rights reserved. No photograph in this publication may be sold to a third party other than in the original form of this publication, or framed for sale to a third party. No parts of this publication may be reproduced, stored in a retrieval system, or transmitted, in any form, or by any means, electronic, mechanical, photocopying, recording or otherwise, without the prior permission of the publishers and copyright holder.

British Library Cataloguing in Publication Data

Coventry - A History and Celebration of the City
David McGrory

The Francis Frith Collection®
Oakley Business Park, Wylye Road,
Dinton, Wiltshire SP3 5EU
Tel: +44 (0) 1722 716 376
Email: info@francisfrith.co.uk
www.francisfrith.com

Printed and bound in Great Britain
Contains material sourced from responsibly managed forests

Front Cover: **COVENTRY, BUTCHER'S ROW 1892** 30916At

Additional photographs by CVOne, Paul Baron and David McGrory.
Domesday extract used in timeline by kind permission of
Alecto Historical Editions, www.domesdaybook.org.

Aerial photographs reproduced under licence from
Simmons Aerofilms Limited.
Historical Ordnance Survey maps reproduced under licence from
Homecheck.co.uk

*The colour-tinting in this book is for illustrative purposes only,
and is not intended to be historically accurate*

AS WITH ANY HISTORICAL DATABASE, THE FRANCIS FRITH ARCHIVE IS
CONSTANTLY BEING CORRECTED AND IMPROVED, AND THE PUBLISHERS
WOULD WELCOME INFORMATION ON OMISSIONS OR INACCURACIES

Contents

6   Timeline

8   Chapter 1 : From Coventry's Beginnings to the 15th Century

28   Chapter 2 : From the 16th to the 18th Century

62   Chapter 3 : The 19th Century

84   Chapter 4 : The 20th Century

110   Chapter 5 : Now and the Future

117   Acknowledgements and Bibliography

121   Free Mounted Print Offer

COVENTRY FROM THE AIR 1958 AFA71238

COVENTRY – *a history and celebration of the city*

Historical Timeline for Coventry

Roman Britain | Dark Ages

- **AD61** Lunt Fort constructed
- **383** Burial of Roman hoard in Foleshill, after fall of Magnus Maximus
- **700** Possible founding of St Osburga's

- **49BC** Julius Caesar crosses the Rubicon
- **AD79** Eruption of Vesuvius destroying Pompeii
- **AD122** Emperor Hadrian orders Hadrian's Wall to be built
- **AD455** Vandals sack Rome
- **AD520** Possible period of King Arthur legend
- **AD871** King Alfred and Danelaw

Tudor Britain | Stuart Britain

- **1539** Coventry Priory suppressed
- **1569** Mary Queen of Scots held in city
- **1642** Charles I attacks Coventry
- **1651** Cromwell in Coventry to stop Prince Charles
- **1678** First Godiva Procession

- **1509** Henry VIII becomes king
- **1558** Accession of Elizabeth 1
- **1588**
- **1600** Founding of East India Company
- **1605** Gunpowder Plot
- **1649** Charles I executed
- **1666** Great Fire of London

Victorian Britain | Edwardian Era

- **1849** Horse Racing in Radford
- **1860** Collapse of the weaving trade
- **1884** The watch trade employs 3,410 people
- **1901** The population of Coventry is 69,978
- **1902** London actress Vera Guedes rides as Lady Godiva
- **1907** Frank Whittle, inventor of the jet engine, born in Coventry
- **1910** Humber establish aeronautical department

- **1837** Victoria becomes queen
- **1846** Repeal of Corn Laws
- **1851** Great Exhibition at Crystal Palace
- **1881** First Boer War
- **1885** Karl Benz designs first automobile
- **1901** Queen Victoria dies
- **1903** Campaign for women's suffrage begins
- **1910** Edward VII dies

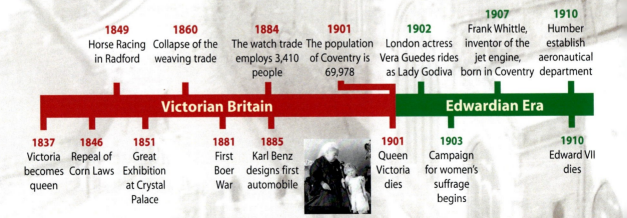

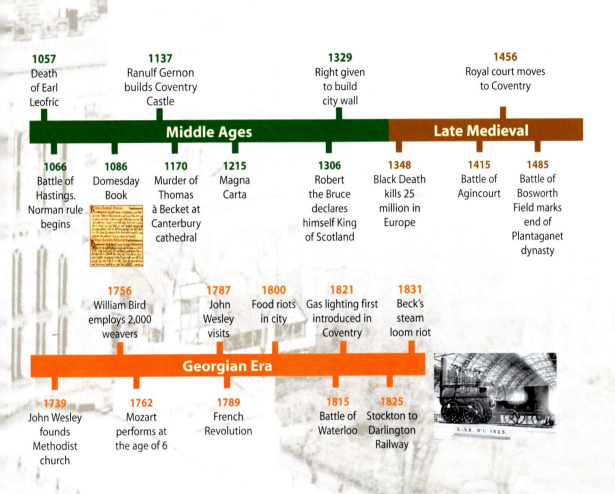
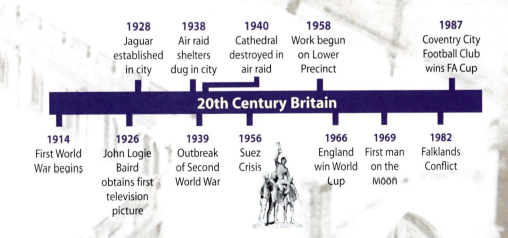

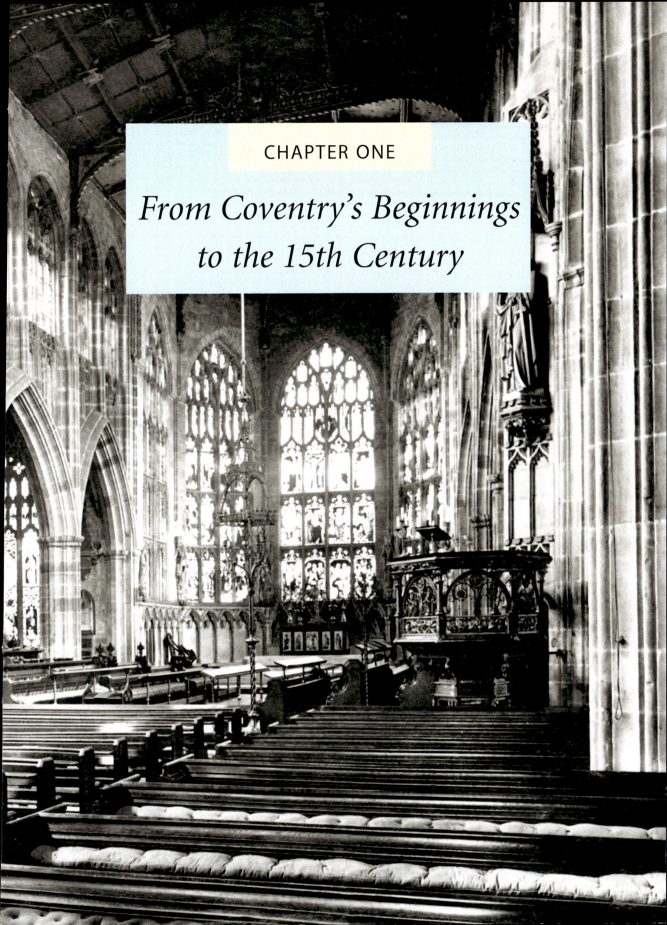

CHAPTER ONE

From Coventry's Beginnings to the 15th Century

THE ORIGINS of Coventry are lost in the mists of time, although some clues have come to light in the past, and more recently too. A few Neolithic worked flint tools have been found, and the Giant's Grave on Primrose Hill appears to be a burial mound. Recently, near Gibbet Hill on the campus of Warwick University, roundhouses from an Iron Age settlement were uncovered. Earlier, Neolithic stone axes which had been brought in to the district from Wales and Cornwall had been found here.

The centre of Coventry itself, namely Broadgate, which stands on the highest hill in the area, was the site of a fascinating discovery in 1947. During the demolition of bombed buildings and preparation for reconstruction, a Bronze Age axe head which dated to 650BC was unearthed by a workman. Later, a second axe came to light amongst the spoil taken from Broadgate, which had been dumped in a field in Canley.

Barr's Hill, the city's second major hill, is also thought to have once been an ancient hill-fort with a covered way leading to a stream. The site was certainly known to the Romans, as coins and pottery have been found here dating from the reign of Tiberius (AD14) to the 4th century. Nearby, Foleshill Road was the site of a major treasure find in 1792 when farmhands digging a ditch unearthed a large pot containing around 1,800 Roman copper coins from the reign of Emperor Constantine onwards. Later, a second pot was discovered, which held more than 2,000 coins.

That a Roman road passed through the centre of Coventry is confirmed by the unearthing of its route at various points. One discovery was reported in the Gentleman's Magazine in 1793: 'In the last summer the street in Coventry, called Broadgate, was opened to a depth of 5 or 6 feet, when a regular pavement was discovered, and upon that pavement, a coin of Nero in middle brass'. Other Roman finds include two small statues (of Mars and a warrior), coins, pottery, brooches, rings, and horseshoes.

On the edge of present-day Coventry stand the excavated remains of a large Roman fort known as the Lunt. This cavalry fort contained a granary and a gyrus, a battle-conditioning ring for horses, the only one known in western Europe. The fort appears to have been in use over various periods between AD60 and AD260. There appears to have been intensive activity on the site during the rebellion led by Boudicca in AD60, and it is likely that after her final defeat at Mancetter, Celtic horses were brought here for re-conditioning.

Coventry (which has now swallowed up many of its surrounding villages) makes its first real appearance during the Saxon period. Legend says that St Chad came here and built a chapel. This may have been the ancient chapel on Barr's Hill; it was dedicated to St Nicholas, and was demolished after the Dissolution. Around the year 700, St Osburga, known as the Divine Fortress, was abbess over a house of nuns in the centre of Coventry. After her death she was venerated as a saint, and the lake below the nunnery bore the name St Osburg's Pool.

From Coventry's Beginnings to the 15th Century 11

AN ANGLO-SAXON DOORJAMB
ZZZ00396 (Drawing by Neil Cowley)

Discovered in 1934 in Palmer Lane, this most likely came from the nunnery of St Osburga.

The Anglo-Saxon Chronicle records that in 1016 Edric the Traitor led the Danish Cnut into the area, and the Danes 'harried and burned and slew all that they found'. The antiquarian John Rous recorded that 'the Abbey of Nuns at Coventry is destroyed'. Cnut became king, and later restored those religious houses that he had destroyed, including Osburga's, no doubt. This rebuilt church most likely stood on the site of the later church founded or endowed by Leofric and Godiva (Godgifu); this later church, although it was called St Mary's, was also dedicated to St Osburga and contained her relics. Recent excavations on the priory site uncovered a skeleton dating from the 8th to 9th century.

Because practically all of the charters relating to Coventry Priory are forgeries, it is no longer certain if Leofric and Godiva actually founded the church or simply endowed it. The historian John Leland states: 'Kyng Canute the Dane made [a] howes of nunes. Leofrike, Erle of the Marches, turned it in Kyng Edward the Confessor's dayes into a howes of monkes'. This may be true; Leofric and Godiva may have exchanged the nuns for monks, prompted by Godiva, who had been encouraged by her father confessor.

Lady Godiva is now one of the best-known historical characters in the world. This was not so in the Saxon period, when it was her husband Earl Leofric of Mercia who was renowned. He was considered great and wise, and even a saint. Leofric was a soldier, but also an extremely religious man; he aided three kings onto the throne, and his death in 1057 was mourned by all England as his body was buried in great pomp in his church in Coventry. Leofric and Godiva's son Aelfgar succeeded Leofric as Earl of Mercia, and after a short and bloody life he was laid beside his father in Coventry.

Godiva lived to see her granddaughter marry King Harold, Harold's defeat at Hastings, and the fall of Saxon England. She was buried in September 1067 at Evesham Abbey, next to Prior Aefic, her father confessor. This suggests that Godiva may have spent those latter days at Evesham, in a monastic house, as was often the case with widowed noble spouses. Godiva willed that her golden jewelled necklet should be hung around the neck of the statue of the Virgin in Coventry's church.

Lady Godiva's legendary ride was not recorded until 1190, when the monks were cast out of Coventry Priory for assaulting Bishop Nonant. Some of the monks went to St Albans, and there told the story to the chronicler Roger of Wendover, who put it in his 'Flores Historiarum'. Wendover wrote that Godiva, wishing to free the town from 'heavy bondage', with prayers asked her husband to help the town. Leofric is said to have rebuked her and told her not to speak of it again, but Godiva persisted. He finally gave in, and said: 'Mount your horse and ride naked before all the people through the market of the town from one end to the other, and on your return, you shall have your request.'

Wendover says that Godiva loosed her hair so that it covered her body and nothing could be seen but her legs; then, attended by two knights, she rode through the market place. Her ride completed, she returned to Leofric,

This small alabaster statue by William Behnes (1795-1864) stands in a special alcove in the Old Mayoress's Parlour in St Mary's Hall.

THE STATUE OF LADY GODIVA c1900 C169303

who was astonished and granted what she wished. Wendover's account survives only as a 14th-century manuscript; as other manuscripts by him survive, this may not be the original version of the story. One version says that Godiva rode through the market place seen by no one, and Leofric declared it to be a miracle. As a miraculous tale, this would be likely to be told by the monks, and so this version is most likely to be the original one.

> ### Did you know?
>
> The 15th-century oak armoured figure, which has been used to represent Peeping Tom since the 17th century, probably actually portrays St George, and most likely came from Coventry Priory, where a relic of St George was kept. The figure now stands in Cathedral Lanes looking down on Godiva.

The tale itself has changed over the centuries, and still does. One major addition to the story in the 17th century was Peeping Tom (who gave the world a name for someone who steals a look). In this version, Tom was a tailor. When everyone was told to go indoors while the lady rode, Tom peeped out and was struck blind.

It is interesting that up until the mid 19th century the village of Southam, ten miles from Coventry, also had a Godiva procession. This procession may give a clue to where the tale originated. Godiva was represented in that village by a supposed naked white lady, accompanied by a black lady, both on horseback. These two were known as the black and white lady, and presumably represented the two aspects of the goddess. They were draped with lace so they could not be seen, and led around the village and fields by a man wearing a bull mask called Brazen Face. He represented the sun god, a symbol of fertility. This fertility procession no doubt also took place in Coventry in ancient times, and the monks simply added their benefactress to the tale, changing a pagan rite to a miraculous Christian tale of self-sacrifice. Godiva herself, of course, would never have needed to resort to riding naked, or any other penance, for in Saxon England noble women such as she held the power themselves to drop bondage if they wished. Only in the feudal Norman mind could such a tale be created.

During Norman times the church of St Mary and its outbuildings was rebuilt as a massive cathedral church 425 feet long, which became a Mecca for pilgrims in later centuries. One of the most notorious bishops was one Hugh de Nonant, who paid Richard I for the see in 1189. Nonant was a monk-hater: he was recorded as saying that if it was up to him, all monks should be driven from England - and he would prefer them to go to the devil. Nonant took total control over the church. Soon after, an argument broke out between him and the monks; the result was that the monks tried to drop a stone from a tower on him, which killed a monk, and then smashed his head with a crucifix before the high altar and 'contaminated' the church.

COVENTRY – *a history and celebration of the city*

ST MARY'S HALL 1892 30929

Since 1678 it was from here that most Godiva processions began. In the courtyard is a stone called Godiva's mounting block, which the old Godiva impersonators used to mount their horses.

From Coventry's Beginnings to the 15th Century 15

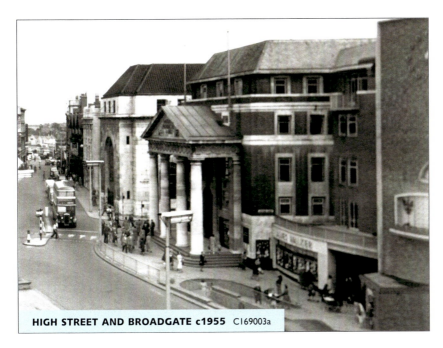

HIGH STREET AND BROADGATE c1955 C169003a

Here we see the NatWest Bank (with the columns) and Lloyd's Bank. When the NatWest was built in 1930, remains of ancient stonework and wooden buildings thought to date to the 12th century were found. When the Lloyds site was dug in 1932, an ancient stone lamp in the Roman style was found, together with large quantities of glazed medieval pottery and shoes from the 12th to the 16th century.

The monks were expelled, and Nonant continued to oppress the people as a supporter of King John. When King Richard returned, Nonant was dismissed from his see; later, on his deathbed, still hoping for a place in heaven, he confessed his many sins before a group of astonished abbots and friars.

In this period Coventry also acquired its first castle, which was built by Ranulf Gernon, Earl of Chester. This castle was attacked by Robert Marmion of Tamworth, to whom Gernon had promised Coventry; but Gernon reneged on his promise. Marmion cast the monks from the priory, and fortified it with ditches and mantraps; he himself later fell into one of these mantraps, and while he lay helpless, he was decapitated by a common foot soldier. Later, after King Stephen had acquired the castle, the Earl of Chester unsuccessfully tried to retake it by building a siege castle against it. The castle was later gained by Gernon's son Hugh Keviloc, who may have been responsible for rebuilding it in stone. Hugh refers to 'the broad gate of my castle' in a charter, thus giving Broadgate in the centre of Coventry its name.

ARTIST'S IMPRESSION OF JOUSTING KNIGHTS
F6017

St Michael's became a cathedral in 1918. The church originated as a chapel built within the bailey of Coventry Castle. Here at Michaelmas 1451 King Henry VI attended high mass after leading a great procession from Coventry Priory. He afterwards gave his gown to the church.

ST MICHAEL'S CHURCH 1892 30923

Hugh rebelled in 1173, and the castle was again attacked and returned to the King by Richard de Lucy. During this attack the castle may have suffered serious damage, which probably led to the decision to make it redundant around 1204, and the land and stonework was gradually sold off. Until the 16th century, the remains of the castle could still be seen behind St Mary's Hall, and the original embattled Caesar's Tower at the back of the hall (which has since been rebuilt) was no doubt a tower of the castle. The hall itself appears to be made of stone robbed from the site, which is surrounded by three defensive ditches. One long-forgotten individual who lived by the castle gate in Broadgate in the 12th century is remembered in an ancient roll: his name was Herman att Castle Gate. After the castle fell out of use, the Earl of Arundel, who had inherited the estate through his wife, built Cheylesmore Manor House, a moated royal residence; its gatehouse is now used as Register office. The manor would later pass into the royal family through Queen Isabella and the Black Prince.

Did you know?

Next to St Mary's Hall stands Castle Yard; it used to be called White Horse Yard, named after an inn which stood on this spot. An excavation was carried out here, and the castle bakehouse was discovered. The yard was mentioned in 1410-11, when it was referred to as the 'castelbachous'.

ST MICHAEL'S CHURCH, THE INTERIOR c1884 17122

The castle ditch runs under the high altar of St Michael's.

ST MICHAEL'S CHURCH, THE INTERIOR 1892 30925

At the time of the destruction of the castle, much of the central street pattern had been laid out, with the two main routes crossing in Broadgate. Commerce grew in the city when a market was established in Cross Cheaping and Broadgate, which then formed a large open triangle in front of the priory. This was originally administered jointly by the prior and the Earl of Chester, and then solely by the prior. The Earl of Chester encouraged more trade in the city by giving new merchants two years free of dues. Because the priory held most of north Coventry, and the Earl the southern half, the two sides are later referred to as the Earl's and Prior's Halves. This had changed by 1250, when the priory was given much of the Earl's land.

From Coventry's Beginnings to the 15th Century

St Michael's and the Bottoners

The tower and spire of St Michael's is the third tallest in England. St Michael's began as a chapel within the bailey of Coventry Castle. After the castle was demolished, the chapel remained, and it was gradually expanded and rebuilt. The great rebuilding of the 14th century was recalled in a verse engraved on a plaque which could once be seen in the church. This commemorated the wealthy Bottoner family, and read:

'William and Adam built the tower,
Ann and Mary built the spire;
William and Adam built the church,
Ann and Mary built the quire.'

The restoration of the tower and spire, which had worn down by time, was completed in 1887; it was refaced with Runcorn sandstone and refilled with new statues, amongst which can be seen members of the Bottoner family.

ST MICHAEL'S CHURCH 1892 30922

THE OLD CATHEDRAL AND HOLY TRINITY CHURCH c1955 C169502

From Coventry's Beginnings to the 15th Century 21

HOLY TRINITY CHURCH 2004 ZZZ0152 (Reproduced by kind permission of Holy Trinity Church)

The amazing Doom Painting recently uncovered and restored in Holy Trinity Church is described as 'one of the most important discoveries ever made in the field of medieval art'. It is believed that the Doom (a depiction of Judgment Day) was painted around 1435, a few years after an earthquake shook Coventry.

In 1329 King Edward III gave the prior and men of Coventry the right to tax goods sold in the market for six years; this was to fund the building of a city wall. Nothing happened until 1356, when the city annals record that 'Richard Stoke, the mayor, laid the first stone at Newgate, and there began the Town Wall'. The building of the wall began in a clockwise direction, and eventually reached the south entrance to the city in 1385. Here King Richard II gave stone from a local quarry on condition that the wall encompassed the royal manor house of Cheylesmore. Work continued on the 2½-mile-long wall, which had five main gates over the main entrances and seven minor gates on the smaller roads. Over time, up to 32 square and round towers were added, which were used for storage and defence. The wall was probably completed well before 1462, although it had some later rebuilding work done.

During these early years, royalty often came to the city, including William the Conqueror, King John, Edward II, Edward III, the Black Prince and Richard II. Richard came in 1385 to lay the foundation stone of the house of

CHEYLESMORE MANOR 2004 C169712k (Paul Baron)

This is the gatehouse of Cheylesmore manor house, a royal residence and now England's oldest Register office. The main half-timbered stone-based building stood behind this gate set within a moat.

the Carthusians. He was back again in 1398 to watch over a duel to the death on Gosford Green between the dukes of Norfolk and Hereford, who had accused each other of treason. On that day the green was surrounded by thousands of sightseers and also thousands of troops and archers. As both men went in for the attack, the contest was stopped, and after a long deliberation they were both exiled. Henry Bolingbroke, the Duke of Hereford, would later return and take the throne for himself as King Henry IV.

On 6 October 1404 Henry IV summoned a parliament to be held in Coventry Priory. Because of its lack of lawyers, this later became known as the 'Lack Learning Parliament'. Henry and his fellow nobles called for the church to start paying taxes, but Thomas of Arundel, the Archbishop of Canterbury, argued that the realm would be in spiritual danger if the church was deprived of some of its vast income. Arundel dropped on his knees before the parliament saying that to deprive the church would be the most heinous sin a

From Coventry's Beginnings to the 15th Century

Alders was once Owen Owen. Underneath the site of the building was an ancient quarry, which in 1936 was shown to contain the remains of what was thought to be an equally ancient farmhouse and cattle shed.

OWEN OWEN c1965 C169126

prince could do. His plea worked, and Henry agreed to gather his money from elsewhere.

The great hero Henry V, who was made a member of the Trinity Guild in St Mary's Hall, came to the city in 1421, and received the customary gift of a golden cup and 100 marks. However, it was his son King Henry VI who became the city's most important royal visitor. Henry came to Coventry for the first time in 1434 as a small boy, probably with his guardian Richard Beauchamp, the Earl of Warwick. In September 1451 Henry returned, and was met by 'the mayor, being then Richard Boys, and his worthy brethren, arrayed in scarlet, and all the commonalty clad in green gowns and red hoods, in Hazelwood beyond the Broad Oak, on horseback attending the coming of our sovereign lord'. Henry stayed at the priory, and before leaving gave the city the rare honour of conferring on it the status of county; thereafter Coventry became the city and county of Coventry, separate from Warwickshire, and remained so until 1842. It was also probably on this visit that Henry was also inducted as a member of Coventry's powerful guild of the Holy Trinity, which was based in St Mary's Hall.

During the time leading to the War of the Roses Henry VI's queen, Margaret of Anjou, fearing that Henry's downfall was being plotted by the Duke of York, persuaded him to retreat to the safety of walled, loyal, Lancastrian Coventry. An assembly was held here, and the Duke of York was expelled from his protectorship. Things got worse, and in September 1456 the entire royal court left London to the supporters of the Yorkist party and moved lock, stock and

Henry VI

COVENTRY TAPESTRY
ZZZ00399 (Craig Taylor)

Henry VI in the Coventry Tapestry in St Mary's Hall.

Henry VI first came to Coventry as a boy in June 1434 with the Earl of Warwick, when he was presented with a large silver-gilt cup. In December 1437 he visited again, and became a regular visitor, and then a resident. Henry was an extremely pious man, and spent much of his time studying the Bible and praying. He also probably suffered from catatonic schizophrenia, and for months would literally just shut down. Others took advantage of this, and thus began the Wars of the Roses. Henry was imprisoned in the Tower, set free, and then imprisoned a second time. Within days of Edward IV's victorious entry into London, Henry was said to have been murdered by Richard of Gloucester, later Richard III.

barrel to Coventry, making the city the new capital of England. The royal court was based in Coventry for nearly three years, and here held parliaments, great councils and royal processions. One parliament became known as the Parliamentum Diabolicum - the Parliament of Devils - for at this parliament twenty-three Yorkist nobles were declared traitors and attainted, losing their rights as nobles and their lands. This sentence was announced from the priory steps.

Henry saw his loyal city for the last time on 5 July 1460, when he left Margaret and his son, Prince Edward, within the safety of its strong walls. He and Margaret exchanged rings. Margaret herself would later be brought as a prisoner to Coventry, and there stand before Edward IV, who had usurped her husband and had been present at the murder of her beloved son. Margaret is said to have rained down curses on Edward's head, which for one moment made him consider executing her. As Edward rode in triumph into London, King Henry VI was murdered in the Tower. This, however, would not be the last time that the people of England or Coventry would hear of him.

MARGARET OF ANJOU, THE COVENTRY TAPESTRY
ZZZ00398 (Craig Taylor)

In the King's Window above the tapestry four kings are depicted with Margaret's badge in the background, as they are all connected to the House of Anjou. Another connection with Anjou is the chained swan in the ceiling of the hall; this was a badge that Margaret personally handed out to her knights.

GOSFORD GATE ZZZ00406 (David McGrory Collection)

It was outside this gate that the army of Edward IV camped, and where he demanded entrance. The site of the gate is now marked in the roadway in Gosford Street.

From Coventry's Beginnings to the 15th Century

Did you know?

On 29 March 1471 Edward IV camped with his army outside Coventry and demanded entrance from Richard Neville, Earl of Warwick. The Earl refused, so Edward left, only to return on 5 April with a larger force. Warwick still refused him entrance, and Edward left for London. The Earl of Warwick left Coventry soon after with a force of 30,000 men, and was killed at Barnet; Edward retook the throne of England.

This ancient pair of stocks stood outside St Mary's Hall. They can now be seen in the museum.

THE STOCKS c1890 C169302

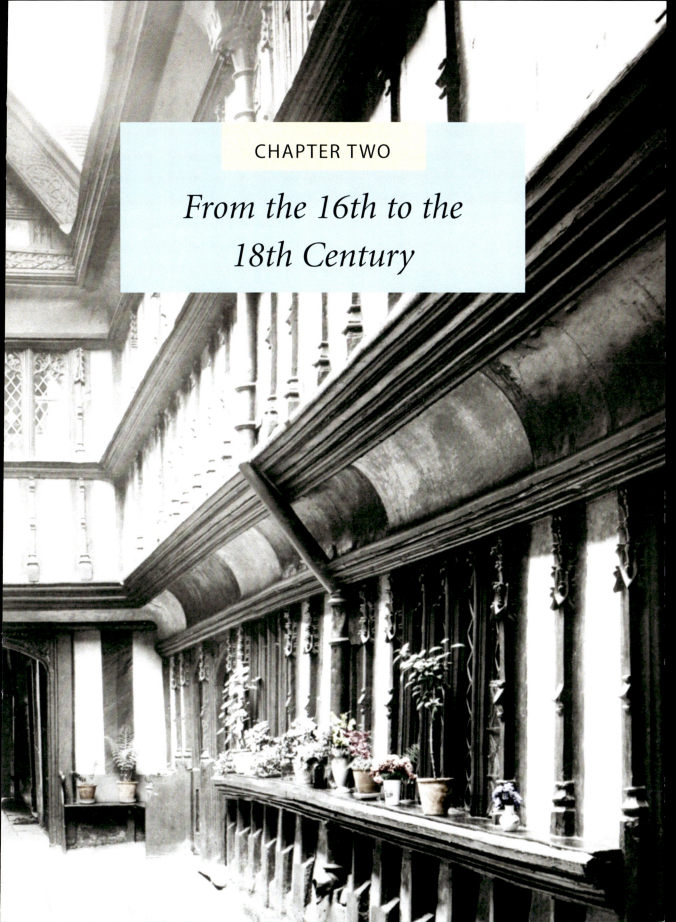

CHAPTER TWO

From the 16th to the 18th Century

KING HENRY VII came to Coventry straight from his victorious battle against Richard III at Bosworth in 1485. The King stayed in the Black Bull Inn in Smithford Street (half way down the present Upper Precinct on the left). He held a council in Coventry Priory, at which all lords were threatened with excommunication if they failed to support his right. Thomas Harrington, a noted Yorkist, was captured and brought to Coventry with Henry, who watched from the Bull as he was beheaded on the Bull Conduit, opposite.

COVENTRY 2004 C169756k (Paul Baron)

Smithford Street

THE WHITE LION, SMITHFORD STREET 1954 ZZZ00401 (Trevor Pring)

We are looking down through the Upper Precinct. The White Lion on the right was the scene of a double murder in 1734. Behind stands Marks & Spencer, built upon the site of the Bull Conduit on which Harrington was beheaded. The Black Bull Inn stood opposite and just above. The original Smithford Street runs downhill towards St John's Church in Fleet Street.

From the 16th to the 18th Century 31

FORD'S HOSPITAL, GREYFRIARS LANE 1892 30917

In the late 19th century, just across the road from here workmen unearthed a purse containing gold coins from the reign of Henry VII.

Henry VII's constant demand for taxes did not help to sustain his popularity; Henry VI's reputation, however, was another story, for in the 1490s the now long-dead king had become the most venerated man in England. After his death, miracles were said to have began to take place at his grave, and the people flocked to the shrine of 'Saint Henry of Windsor'. Henry VII claimed that St Henry had prophesied his coming, and used this to legitimise his claim to the throne. He had a list compiled of 300 miracles and 174 wonders, which was sent to the Vatican as evidence for Henry's canonization, and began to build his great chapel at Westminster to house Henry's uncorrupted body.

It was during these peak years of Henry VI's veneration in the 1490s that members of the Trinity Guild, of which Henry was twice installed a member, and members of the council, must have decided to create their own shrine to Henry in St Mary's Hall. The great north window was shortened and a new window created which mirrors the shrine to Henry in York, showing Henry and his ancestors back to Constantine the Great and King Arthur. This window, called the King's Window, would have been considered a shrine to Henry; if they wished his help, people could pray to the image of the saintly Henry in the centre. Outside the hall, niches were created in which statues were placed mirroring the images inside.

FORD'S HOSPITAL IN GREYFRIARS LANE 1892 J0910

From the 16th to the 18th Century

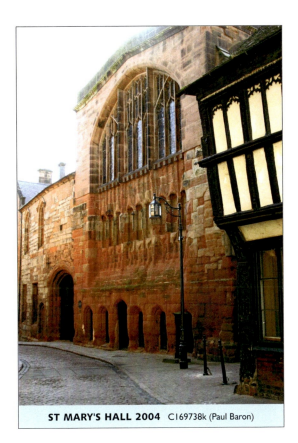

ST MARY'S HALL 2004 C169738k (Paul Baron)

SAINT HENRY OF WINDSOR, THE KING'S WINDOW
ZZZ01524 (David McGrory)

The space below the window was filled with a 30ft-long tapestry, the Coventry Tapestry. This tapestry shows Henry VI looking upon a vision of the annunciation of the Virgin, which he had seen when he was alive; he also wears thick chains, symbolic of his imprisonment before his murder. His queen, Margaret of Anjou, also appears, wearing mourning jewellery, and numerous members of the royal court are shown, including John Talbot, Earl of Shrewsbury and Cardinal Beaufort, the king's uncle. The tapestry not only depicts the veneration of Henry as a saint, but also commemorates Coventry's greatest moment when it became home to the royal court. All the figures pictured lived for some time in Coventry, and had been to feasts and ceremonies in the Guildhall. The ceiling of the Guildhall also acquired a huge number of chained antelopes, the badge of Henry VI, and chained swans, a badge used by Margaret and their son Prince Edward. This hall is the most important relic of the veneration of Henry VI left in England.

THE GREAT HALL, ST MARY'S HALL INTERIOR 1892 30931

This was once home to the Trinity Guild and the council. At the end of the hall is the Coventry Tapestry and the King's Window, celebrating Coventry's greatest moment when it was home to a royal saint.

HOLY TRINITY CHURCH c1968 C169139

The pulpit, thought to be the highest in England, is decorated with two heads, said to be those of Henry VI and Margaret of Anjou.

At this time Coventry was full of religious houses. They were the Benedictine priory (whose ruins stand in Priory Row and New Buildings); Greyfriars, home of the Franciscans (the tower and spire stand off New Union Street); Whitefriars, home of the Carmelites (off London Road); and Charterhouse, home of the Carthusians, on London Road. Other religious foundations included the old Grammar School, then known as the Hospital of St John. Coventry Priory became a popular place of pilgrimage, for it held the arm of St Augustine, the head of St Osburga, a relic of St George and a phial of the milk of the Virgin, plus numerous other relics of saints and barrels of minor relics. Another popular place with pilgrims was the famed Tower of Our Lady, which was in fact a tower within the city wall by London Road with a statue and a painted chamber.

> ## Did you know?
>
> *In medieval times, the first inn outside New Gate and on London Road was the Salutation. It is said that the inn got this name because as people left the city they saluted the Tower of Our Lady in the belief that it would protect them on their journey.*

Coventry was full of monks and friars; some were popular, like the grey friars (the Franciscans), and some were not so, like the Benedictines of St Mary's Priory. When Henry VIII wished to remarry, he split from Rome and created the Church of England. He enriched his coffers through the Dissolution, which began in Coventry in 1538 with the dissolution of Greyfriars and Whitefriars (the house of the Carmelites). The grey friars surrendered to the Crown on 5 October 1538, and their guardian John Stafford wrote: 'with like mutual assent and consent [we] do surrender and yield up into the hands of the same, all our said House of Saint Francis'. The King's Commissioner, Doctor Loudon, send in men to destroy the church and outbuildings. His reason, which he reported to his master Thomas Cromwell, was because 'the poor people lay so sore upon it'.

From the 16th to the 18th Century 37

THE CLOISTERS, WHITEFRIARS 2004 ZZZ01525 (CVOne)

This is one of the largest surviving examples of a Carmelite house in England. After being the private residence of the Hales family, in 1801 it became a workhouse, and the cloister was used as the inmates' dining room.

Once Henry had taken the smaller monasteries, he looked to the great ones, which included the priory of St Mary. In 1538 he planned to take the priory, which he himself had visited a few years earlier. The prior pleaded for the house, and so did the Bishop, Roland Lee, who had supported Henry in his split from Rome and his subsequent marriage, which he performed. Thomas Cromwell promised Lee that his church would survive, but despite this Doctor Loudon came to Coventry with papers for its destruction. Lee agued his case, and Loudon wrote back to Cromwell asking if the church should be suppressed or made secular. Cromwell, however, had decided to let the other diocesan church of Lichfield stand and to suppress Coventry.

The monks were promised pensions, most of which were never paid, and the building was stripped of its relics, which were transported to the Tower of London and there burnt in the street. The great scriptorium (the library) was also stripped, and its volumes were sold to be used as ships' ballast and firelighters. The priory lay empty, and locals began to smash its windows and to take away stone to incorporate into their houses. The buildings were becoming ruinous, and wild dogs took up residence there, feeding off the offal dumped in the ruins by the local butchers of nearby Great Butcher Row.

WHITEFRIARS, THE GATEWAY 2004 C169717k (Paul Baron)

The buildings were sold in June 1545, and then in the following month passed into the hands of John Combe and Richard Stansfield, who may have started their final destruction. The priory then passed into the hands of John Hales, a baronet and Clerk of the Hanaper, who took up residence in Coventry and converted the old Whitefriars monastery into his home, Hales Place.

The area below the white building (middle right) was called the Bull Ring because in 1424 it was ordained by the Leet that all bulls should be baited here in front of the priory gate before they were slaughtered by the local butchers.

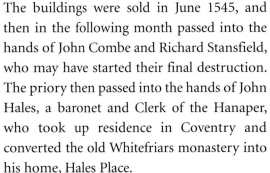

LOOKING DOWN GREAT BUTCHER ROW INTO THE BULL RING 1892 30918a

From the 16th to the 18th Century

BUTCHER ROW 1892 C169001

VIEW FROM BROADGATE TOWARDS TRINITY STREET 2004 C169754k (Paul Baron)

From the 16th to the 18th Century 41

As for the priory church itself, what remained of the lead was stripped from the roof, and a stone and soil ramp was made down the main steps into the building. Down this ramp went wagons, to be loaded with the stonework, wood, metal work and floor tiles stripped from the interior. During later excavation work it was still possible to see the wheel ruts made inside the building. When the work was completed, little remained but some walls, the west entrance and the cross aisle; here in the 17th century a private house, Tower House, was built by the Rev John Bryan. After it was systematically stripped, the site was later sold to the council for £400. The document of sale describes it as 'the site of the late monastery of Our Lady the Virgin, aforesaid together with the dye house, water mill and leet'.

The school was built in 1856 over the west entrance to Coventry Priory. The building in the background stands above the surviving basement of one of the entrance towers. The main entrance to the priory was between the columns on the left.

THE BLUE COAT SCHOOL FOR GIRLS 1890 C169301

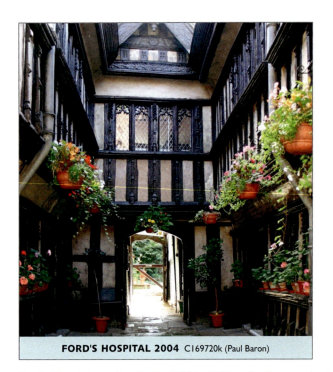

FORD'S HOSPITAL 2004 C169720k (Paul Baron)

The wholesale destruction of Coventry's monastic houses had an effect on the local economy, and many people, possibly thousands, left the city. This was not, however, simply because of the Dissolution; the exodus was also due to the decline in the cloth and cap trade. Coventry was particularly noted for its dark blue dyed thread and cloth, which was so strong and long-lasting that it bore the name 'Coventry True Blue'. John Hales wrote: 'I have heard say that the chief trade at Coventry was heretofore in making of blue thread, and then the town was rich … now our thread comes all from beyond sea. Whereforto that trade of Coventry is decayed, and thereby the town likewise.'

Ford's Hospital was founded in 1509 by William Ford, a merchant who left instructions that it was for 'six poor men and their wives'. By the 18th century it was exclusively for women.

FORD'S HOSPITAL 2004 C169719k (Paul Baron)

In 1547 King Edward VI continued the Reformation. Under his reforms, the city merchant guilds of the Holy Trinity and Corpus Christi were dissolved. The churches that served these guilds - St John's in Fleet Street and St Nicholas' in St Nicholas Street, Radford - were closed. St Nicholas', possibly one of the earliest churches in the city, was eventually demolished sometime after 1610. St John's became many things, such as a winding house and a prison, before, in 1734, it was finally returned to being a parish church.

Religious intolerance also eventually brought to an end the nationally famed Coventry Mystery Plays, which were performed at the feast of Corpus Christi by the many trade guilds; the plays brought thousands of visitors to the city, including the nobility. The day began with the guilds and aldermen and churchmen taking part in a torchlight procession. Then the plays were performed on moveable pageant wagons sited around the city. The plays began at dawn with the creation and continued until nightfall

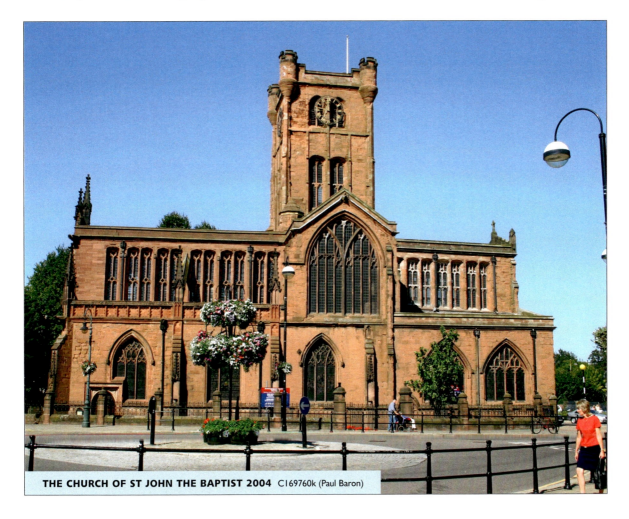

THE CHURCH OF ST JOHN THE BAPTIST 2004 C169760k (Paul Baron)

The church itself is built upon huge oak piles driven into the bed of an ancient lake, 'Babbu lacu'. This lake has occasionally risen in the past, and the interior of the church has been under six feet of water. Set into the wall of the building on the left can still be seen a piece of the old city wall; at this point stood Spon Street Gate with its towers and battlements.

From the 16th to the 18th Century 45

BOND'S HOSPITAL 2004 C169767k (Paul Baron)

Bond's Hospital was founded by Thomas Bond in 1507. The courtyard was shared with Bablake School, a school that appears to have already existed on the site at that time.

with doomsday - the damned were dragged screaming into the flaming hell's mouth by devils, just before the end of the world. In 1589 there were calls to ban the 'papist' plays, and eventually they were replaced by a more puritanical play called 'The Destruction of Jerusalem'. The play was a flop, as it held none of the spectacle and humour of the original mysteries. The following year other plays were added to it, but none cared for them; thus the famed Coventry Mystery Plays were not seen again until their revival in the late 20th century.

During the 16th century, the nation's changeable religious habits had far more sinister results. In the year 1510 Henry VIII himself stayed in Coventry Priory, and in that same year ten Lollards (who believed that God should be celebrated in English and not Latin) were made to carry large faggots, symbols of their deaths by fire, through the market place. The symbolic act worked, for all recanted except for Joan Ward; she suffered for her belief by being burned at the stake in the Park Hollows. In 1519 Alice Lansdail, along with Thomas, her brother-in-law, Hosea Hawkins, Thomas Wrexham, Robert Hockett and Thomas Bond, suffered the same horrific fate by order of the Bishop of Coventry, Geoffrey Blyth. One man, Robert Silksby, escaped only to be taken again and 'cleansed' in the flaming pit.

From the 16th to the 18th Century

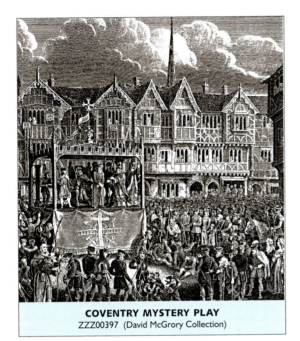

COVENTRY MYSTERY PLAY
ZZZ00397 (David McGrory Collection)

Christ stands before Pilate in the Coventry Mystery Plays in Broadgate in the 16th century. The pageant wagons were towed around the city by horses, and the players changed below in the curtained-off area. When not in use, the companies kept the wagons in buildings called pageant houses.

The Church of England reigned until Edward VI's death and the ascension of Mary Tudor, better known as 'Bloody Mary'. Under her the Catholic faith was restored, causing problems for those who worshipped under the Protestant faith. One who found the change difficult was Lawrence Saunders, Rector of All Hallows, Bread Street, in London; he continued to worship as a Protestant, and was accused of heresy and sent to Coventry in 1555 to be 'purified' by the fire. He was followed by Robert Glover of Manchester, who was taken instead of his brother and burned without evidence against him. The next victim was John Careless, who appears to have been a Coventry man. He was well-liked, and was allowed to leave the gaol to appear in the mystery plays. Careless was sent to London accused of heresy, but he cheated the stake by dying in prison. High standing in the community did not help, for Jocelyn Palmer, an Oxford graduate and son of a Coventry mayor, was burned in the Little Park in 1557.

The year 1565 was a better on for the city, for on 17 August the great Virgin Queen, Elizabeth I, arrived. Before she entered through Bishop Gate the mayor presented her with a purse of gold, and with it a pretty speech. The Queen took the purse, saying: 'I thank you, Mr Mayor. I have few such gifts; it is one hundred pounds in gold.' To this the mayor responded: 'May it please your Majesty, there is a great deal more in it.' 'What is that?' said the Queen. 'It is the hearts of all your loving subjects.' 'True, Mr Mayor, it is a great deal more indeed', replied Elizabeth.

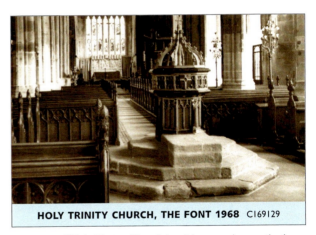

HOLY TRINITY CHURCH, THE FONT 1968 C169129

The font of Holy Trinity Church is said to stand upon the base of Swine's Cross, which stood at the junction of Bishop Street and Silver Street, marking the site of the pig market. From these steps citizens would have stood for a better view of Queen Elizabeth as she passed down the street.

Mary, Queen of Scots was brought to the city late on a November evening in 1569. She and her fifty servants were lodged in Coventry's largest medieval inn, the Black Bull in Smithford Street. Her 'guardians', the Earls of Huntingdon and Shrewsbury, were quickly told by Queen Elizabeth to move the Scottish queen from the 'common inn' to somewhere more suitable, such as Whitefriars. Mary was moved a week later, and spent a day and night at the Old Mayoress's Parlour in St Mary's Hall before being moved into Whitefriars, where she stayed until 2 January 1570.

WHITEFRIARS 2004 ZZZ01532 (CVOne)

Here in the main upstairs room Queen Elizabeth I, Mary Queen of Scots and James I relaxed during their visits to the city. The building is said to be haunted by an inmate who hung herself here in the 19th century, and by Lady Hales, who was killed here by a cannon ball during the siege of Coventry in 1642.

Mary's son King James I came to Coventry on 2 September 1617 and was presented with a huge and highly decorative golden cup containing £100. He feasted in St Mary's Hall and slept at Whitefriars. The Leet Book records that at this time the first self-electing closed council was formed, which nullified ancient rights going back to the reign of Edward III. James's charter, called the Governing Charter of 1621, confirmed the right of the council to become self-governing and self-electing, which it remained until 1835.

Did you know?

In 1641 an inmate of Bond's Hospital called Johnson murdered by poison 12 other inmates, and was buried in the road before Cook Street Gate.

On the eve of the outbreak of the Civil War, an attendant of Charles I recorded in his diary, the 'Iter Carolinum', that the King came to Stoneleigh Abbey on the evening of 19 August 1642. Coventry's Recorder, Spencer Compton, informed him that he would hold the city, and secure the powder magazine in Spon Gate. Things did not go to plan, however, and the powder was taken and moved to Warwick Castle. The City Recorder was panicking, as 400 armed Birmingham men had arrived; after trying to gain more support in the Black Bull Inn, he was forced to flee for his life through the back door into the Bull Yard. He headed straight to Stoneleigh to inform the King.

On the following morning the King sent out a herald to tell of his coming, but was told he could enter with only 200 of his cavaliers. After this insult, the King signed a document of submission and sent it by herald back to Coventry. It reads: 'Whereas diverse persons ill affected to his Majesties person and government, and strangers to this City of Coventry, are lately gotten into that city with arms and ammunition, who, with others of that place ill affected to the peace of this Kingdom, have combined to keep the said city by force of arms against his Majesty, their liege Lord and Sovereign. For reducing of whom to their due obedience his Majesty hath given orders to some Commanders of his Forces to assault the said City, and by force to enter the same. Notwithstanding his Majesty being very unwilling, for some disaffecting persons to punish his good subjects and ruin his said City, is graciously pleased thereby to declare that in case the said Strangers shall forthwith, after the publishing of this His Proclamation, depart peaceably out of the said City and they and the inhabitants presently lay down their arms, that then his Majesty will pardon as well all the said strangers, as well as all the other Inhabitants of the said City. But if they persist in their said Action of Rebellion then his Majesty is resolved to proceed against them as Traitors and Rebels, and to use all extremity for reducing the said City to due Obedience. Given at our Court at Stoneleigh Abbey the twentieth day of August in the eighteenth year of our Reign. 1642.'

What Coventry's answer was is not recorded; but Charles sent to Northampton for siege weapons, and his cannon were set up on Park Hill on the brow of the Little Park quarry. An attack was made against New Gate, and a Parliamentary pamphlet tells us that 'his Majesty continued his siege and battered against the town from Saturday till Monday last. That the cavaliers, with their pieces of ordnance, having battered down one of the gates, the townsmen, to prevent their entrance, stopped up the passage with harrows, carts and pieces of timber, and with great courage forced the cavaliers (notwithstanding their ordnance) upon every attempt towards the gate soon to retreat, and that with the same loss.

GOLDEN CROSS 2004 C169701k (David McGrory)

The 17th-century Golden Cross is said to have been built on the site of the 15th-century mint.

COVENTRY – a history and celebration of the city

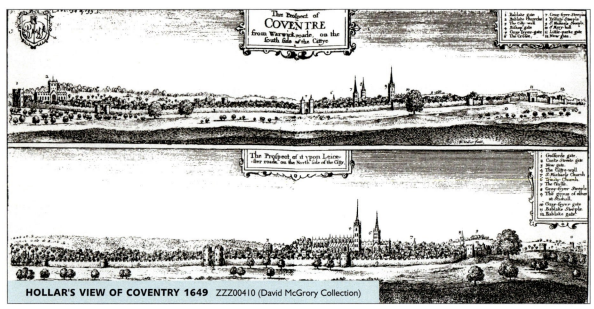

HOLLAR'S VIEW OF COVENTRY 1649 ZZZ00410 (David McGrory Collection)

Charles I's army attacked the walled city at New Gate (top

LYCHGATE COTTAGE 2004 C169702k (David McGrory)

Lychgate Cottage, by Broadgate, was built by Holy Trinity's Rev John Bryan from re-used timbers in 1650.

On the Monday, hearing of the approach of the Parliamentarian forces under Lord Brooke from the south, the King chose to make a withdrawal. He sent a small force to halt Brooke's advance, and three companies of foot and dragoons to hold Kenilworth Castle. Charles himself rode for Nottingham, where he raised the royal standard and there officially began the English Civil War.

Brooke's men marched into Coventry to the sound of a trumpet which had been taken from a cavalier they had killed on the way. With these soldiers was trooper Nehemiah Wharton, who wrote: 'My last was unto you from Coventry, August 26th, which place is still our quarter; a city environed with a wall co-equal, if not exceeding, that of London for breadth and height ... It hath four strong gates, strong battlements, stored with towers ... This city hath magnificent churches and stately streets; within it there are also several and pleasant sweet springs of water, built of free stone, very large, sufficient to supply many thousand men. The city gates are guarded day and night with four hundred armed men, and no man entereth in or out, but upon examination. It is also very sweetly situate. Thursday August 26th. Our soldiers pillaged a malignant fellow's house in the city and the Lord Brooke immediately proclaimed that whosoever should ... offend should have martial law ... Friday several of our soldiers, both horse and foot, sallied out of the city unto the Lord Dunsmore's Park ... and brought from thence great store of venison.'

ST MARY'S HALL, THE CITY ARMOURY 2004
ZZZ01528 (David McGrory)

This is all that remains of the city armoury in St Mary's Hall. Many of these pieces last saw action in the Civil War.

Coventry thereafter came under military rule and became a garrison town. The City Recorder, the cavalier Earl of Northampton, was thrown from office in his absence, and the Parliamentarian general Robert Devereux, Earl of Essex, was given the honour in St Mary's Hall. On 14 October the King's nephew, the flamboyant Prince Rupert of the Rhine, sent a letter to the city demanding its surrender in the King's name. He was refused, and he rode on the city with his cavaliers; but he quickly retreated when he found 26 pieces of ordnance playing upon him.

The city did not feel under major threat

Did you know?

In 1643 the City Annals record that 'The women went in company to fill the quarries in the Great Park, that they might not harbour an enemy. Being called together by a drum they marched together into the Park with mattocks and spades, being led by one goodwife Adderley with an Hercules Club on her shoulder and drew off from work by one Mary Herbert with a pistol in her hand that she shot off when they were dismissed.'

again until 1644, when the King's side appeared to prevail. A head count was taken, and around 9,500 were found to be within the walls. New towers were added, and cannon placed in them. Also, to reduce the population because of food shortage, some people, mainly non-churchgoers and single women, were expelled. No attack came, but the following year, after

Charles took Leicester, the threat returned. The entire city was called out to extend the defences outside Gosford Gate and to protect the city further by re-routing the river. Oliver Cromwell came to Coventry for the first time that year in May, and around this time turned the tide of war with his New Model Army and a victory at Naseby.

In August 1648 a royalist Scottish army was defeated at Preston; several hundred prisoners were sent to Coventry and kept in St John's Church, the Leather Hall, Spon Gate, Greyfriars Gate and other unspecified places. It has been said that when the prisoners who were kept in St John's were exercised in the street, the people snubbed them, thus giving rise to the saying 'sent to Coventry'. However, this explanation dates only from the 19th century; there are other possible explanations, including the fact that in the past people were sent to Coventry to be executed, and therefore would never be spoken to again.

In 1651 Prince Charles (later Charles II) led a Scottish army south. Coventry was re-fortified, and on 25 August Cromwell arrived, followed by an army. As Charles drew nearer, he gained intelligence of the huge Parliamentarian force at Coventry, and turned off towards Worcester. Cromwell marched and destroyed the Royalist force, ending the war.

Cromwell died in 1658 and was succeeded by his unsuccessful son Richard.

THE TOWER OF ST JOHN'S 2004 C169703k (Heather Head)

The embattled tower of St John's peeps over a timbered

The Commonwealth fell, which led to the restoration of Charles II, who landed in England in May 1660. In October James Compton, son of the pre-war City Recorder, rode into Coventry at the head of a large group of Warwickshire gentry; he was duly entertained to a feast in St Mary's Hall, and the following day he was made the new City Recorder. The city fathers, mindful of the new King's feelings towards a Parliamentarian stronghold, made a gift to the King of Cheylesmore manor and park and its rents, which had been taken back by the city during the Commonwealth. They also had a silver ewer and basin specially made, which cost 150 guineas, and added 50 guineas in gold. Despite the city's generosity, Charles was unimpressed, and contemptuously gave Cheylesmore to Sir Robert Townsend. He then ordered the slighting of the wall which had kept his father at bay, and on 22 July 1662 Lord Compton returned to the city with 500 men and began to demolish Coventry's pride, its great city wall, starting symbolically where Charles I had attacked it at New Gate.

It was during the reign of Charles I that the Godiva Procession appears to have begun. The City Annals of 1678 states that 'Att the Great Fair several Companys found a streamer of the Armes of their Companyes & each paraded a follower & the Lady Godiva Rode before the Mayor to proclaim the Fair.' The first to play Godiva was a boy, the son of James Swinnerton; like all early Godivas, he was draped completely in a fly net so that no one could quite see him. As for Peeping Tom, it is

Holy Trinity Church

HOLY TRINITY CHURCH 1892 30927

John Bryan, the Vicar of Holy Trinity during the Civil War, had previously been treasurer of the Parliamentarian army. The tower and spire of Holy Trinity (which is the city's second tallest, measuring 237 feet) fell down during a gale in 1665, killing a small boy. It was rebuilt the following year, and has been repaired on numerous occasions since.

an interesting fact that a certain John Warren recorded in 1659 during the Commonwealth that he saw the figure of Tom leaning from a window by the Coventry Cross.

THE GODIVA PUPPET CLOCK, BROADGATE 2004
C169779k (Paul Baron)

The head of Peeping Tom peers out over Godiva when she rides out on the hour, keeping up the long-established tradition.

Coventry in the 18th century had the feel of a market town. Unlike many other English cities, it had not suffered a great fire, and therefore it looked much the same then as it had 300 years earlier. Most of the city gates still existed, and the street plan was the same as it had been for centuries. Broadgate and Cross Cheaping were still the heart of the city, and weekly markets took place around the nationally famed Coventry Cross. An anonymous writer described Cross Cheaping in 1702, saying that 'This is ye biggest place in ye towne, and ye street very broad, runs off a great length, and most of ye streets are very good. Ye buildings are mostly of timber work and old. There is a Water House at the end of ye town wch springs does supply by pipes ye Town with water ... There is also a water wch serves severall mills that belong to the Town; it seems to be a thriving good trading Town, and is very rich'.

THE GODIVA PUPPET CLOCK IN BROADGATE 2004 C169780k (Paul Baron)

From the 16th to the 18th Century 55

CROSS CHEAPING 1892 30914

Looking down Cross Cheaping towards Bishop Street.

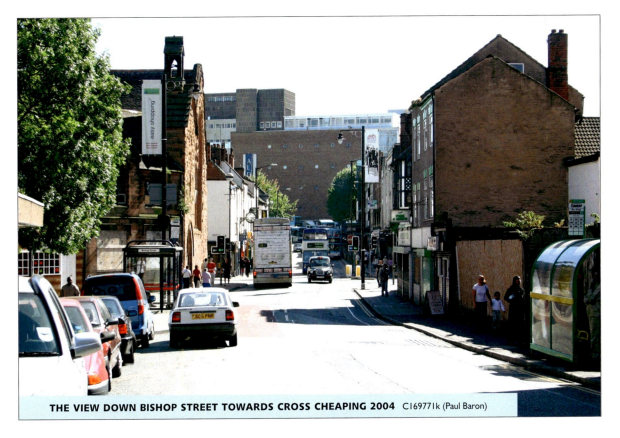

THE VIEW DOWN BISHOP STREET TOWARDS CROSS CHEAPING 2004 C169771k (Paul Baron)

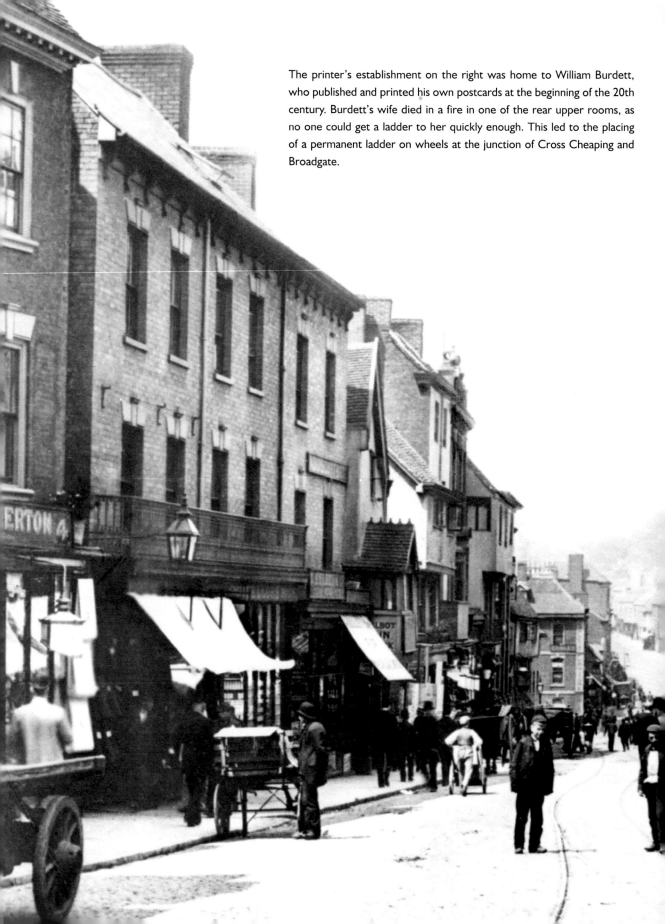

The printer's establishment on the right was home to William Burdett, who published and printed his own postcards at the beginning of the 20th century. Burdett's wife died in a fire in one of the rear upper rooms, as no one could get a ladder to her quickly enough. This led to the placing of a permanent ladder on wheels at the junction of Cross Cheaping and Broadgate.

> ## Did you know?
>
> From at least 1300 the joining point of Cross Cheaping and Broadgate was the site of a cross. The street takes its name from the 'cheaping' market, which was held around the cross. The most famous cross to stand here was the 57-foot Coventry Cross, erected in 1544.

Trades which made Coventry rich were at this time based largely on the manufacture of woollen cloth. The manufacture of worsted cloth was important, for in 1780 William Newly, a worsted weaver, published an apology in the Coventry Mercury for having instructed some Spanish prisoners in the 'art and mystery' of worsted weaving. Another huge trade in 18th-century Coventry was the manufacture of silk ribbons, and by the middle of the century many Coventrians were employed in the silk weaving trade. Thomas Bird, who died in 1746, is alone recorded as employing 2,000 people in the trade. Thomas Pennant records in 1782 an estimated 10,000 employed in the silk weaving trade.

The only mulberry tree in Coventry stands off Spon Street; it is believed to be a survival of an 18th-century attempt to produce silk in the city. The silk worms ate only mulberry leaves.

THE OLD MULBERRY TREE 2004 C169764k (Paul Baron)

Although clock making had been established in the city by Samuel Watson, Mathematician in Ordinary to Charles II in the late 17th century, the 18th century saw the sustained rise in the manufacture of pocket watches with firms such as Rotherham's in Spon Street.

Political elections in Coventry during the 18th century became a national scandal, and were finally controlled by an act of parliament. Daniel Defoe tells us that in 1706 'The Mob of Coventry headed by Sir Chr. Ha-s [Sir Christopher Hales] and Mr G-y [Grey], having at the last Election beaten the Magistrates, wounded the Mayor, disarm'd the Watch-men, and taken away their Halberts, and so carried on the most violent Tumult, that has been seen in this Nation for many years; and under the influence of it, made a pretended Election of the said Sir Chr. H-s

> ## Did you know?
>
> In 1764 a Mr Arnould, late of Coventry, exhibited to King George III a watch so small it could fit on a ring.

PRIORY ROW 2004 C169705k (David McGrory)

This is one of the Georgian houses built in Priory Row on top of the remains of Coventry Priory.

and Mr G-y. To back their Proceedings, they indicted the Mayor and Magistrates, and some of the Citizens for a Riot.'

The riotous election of 1780 became known as the 'Bludgeon Fight'. It began when the mayor Thomas Pickin swore in 66 non-eligible freemen, giving them the right to vote. This common practice of swearing in false freeman gave the mayor's party self-created voters who became known as 'mushroom freemen', because they popped up out of the shadows overnight. Handbills were spread around the city saying 'Mushrooms, Take Care'; they listed 150 false freemen sworn in by the mayor. These included a silk weaver from London and soldiers serving in Portsmouth.

The Corporation employed several hundred 'colliers, roughs and prize-fighters', and gathered them at St Mary's Hall to arm them with staves. These men came under the guise of special constables, 'keeping the peace'. They were told to keep control of the voting booth, which they tried to do against a similar armed mob that had already taken the booth. A bloody street fight ensued, until 'the Yellows [Whigs] were driven back ... The Blues [Tories] chased some of the colliers into St Mary's Hall, where stone throwing commenced, and a considerable quantity of old and valuable [15th-century] stain glass was destroyed.' The corruption of the mushroom freemen and the armed mobs was finally put down by an Act of Parliament called the Coventry Act early in the following century.

A SKETCH OF ST MARY'S HALL
ZZZ00409 (David McGrory Collection)

St Mary's Hall was the centre of government and politics in the city. Here 'mushroom freemen' were sworn in, and election mobs armed. The 15th-century stained glass windows on the left were smashed in the 1780

From the 16th to the 18th Century

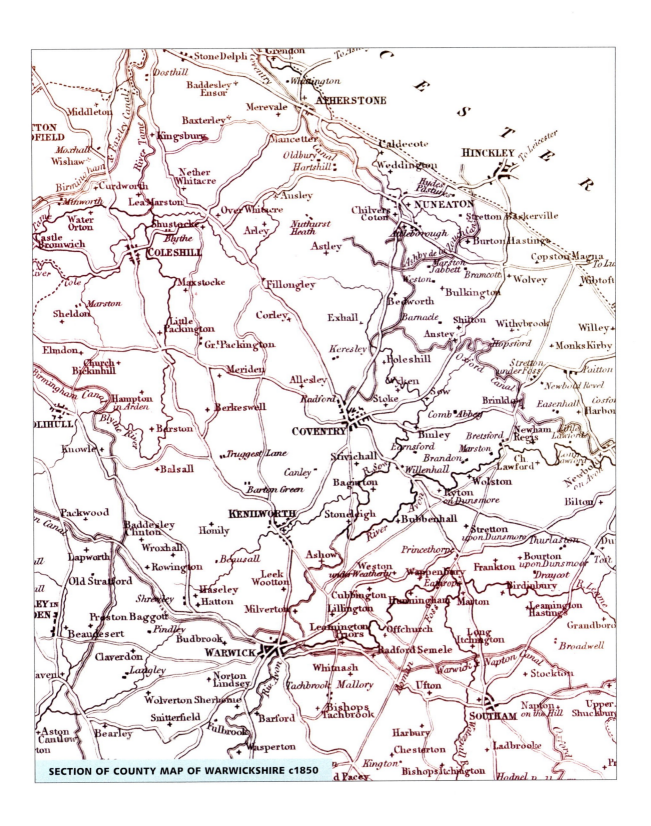

SECTION OF COUNTY MAP OF WARWICKSHIRE c1850

CHAPTER THREE

The 19th Century

AN ANONYMOUS early 19th-century writer wrote that 'Coventry has three spires, one of pre-eminent beauty, and the others deficient in attraction, only from a comparison with St Michael's. They rise high in the air and prepare the approaching traveller for an entrance to a place of great population, and striking architectural importance. The entrances however are uniformly mean and bad; and a person accustomed to contemplate the improved buildings of recent periods looks in vain for the anticipated affluence of domestic architecture. The streets are very narrow, and the footways are formed of sharp, pebbly stones ... it presents the aspect of a city of the 16th century, the upper parts of the houses projecting as was customary'.

THE THREE SPIRES 1890 C169002

This is the classic view of the three spires across Greyfriars Green; this was perhaps the most favoured view on sale around the city. The churches are (left to right) Holy Trinity, St Michael's and Christchurch (Greyfriars). The perspective between Holy Trinity (left) and St Michael's is always strange from here, as the two churches, which are very close, appear to be a good distance apart.

The 19th Century 65

66 COVENTRY – *a history and celebration of the city*

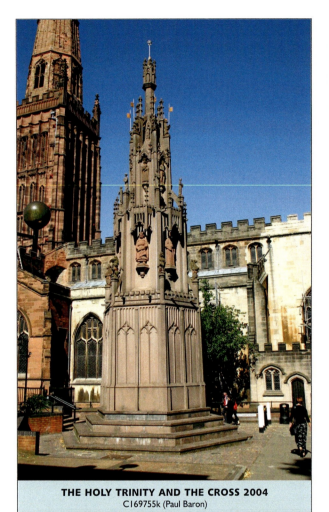

THE HOLY TRINITY AND THE CROSS 2004
C169755k (Paul Baron)

Here we see a reconstruction of Coventry Cross, with Holy Trinity in the background. Here, just by the cross, the last public hanging took place in 1849.

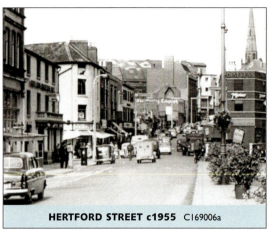

HERTFORD STREET c1955 C169006a

The first building on the left (which has now gone) was the original Three Tunns Inn. This began life as a coaching inn; it closed in 1965. In the upper window of the white building behind there used to be one of the city's Peeping Tom images, a head and shoulders copy of the original figure.

This comment was true, for little major construction in the city dated from the 'recent periods' the writer so favoured. The exceptions were the County Hall, which still stands in Cuckoo Lane, built in 1783, the barracks, built in 1793, and now gone, and some Georgian town houses, which can still be seen in Little Park Street and Priory Row.

The beginning of the 19th century brought a few street improvements with the demolition of the west side of Broadgate in 1820 to make a truly broad street. The south entrance, Greyfriars Lane, remained a bottleneck until one day in 1807. The Prince Regent was on his way to Coombe Abbey, and when his carriage came down the lane its passage was inevitably delayed. The Prince said to the Marquis of Hertford: 'I hope, my Lord, the good people of Coventry will make their streets wider before I come here again.' In 1811-12 an Act of Parliament to improve the streets of Coventry was passed, and a new street was laid on land belonging to the lord of Cheylesmore manor, the Marquis of Hertford; the street became known as Hertford Street in his honour. When the Prince passed through again a few years later, he was said to have been much pleased with

HERTFORD STREET 2004 C169722k (Paul Baron)

VIEW OF COVENTRY BY HENRY JEAYES 1809 ZZZ00408 (David Morgan)

This view shows St Michael's on the left and Holy Trinity on the right.

the new road. Another major road cut from the bottom of Spon Street was Holyhead Road, a toll road created by Thomas Telford between 1827 and 1830.

Over the centuries Coventry had been held within its ancient boundaries in a stranglehold of lands known as Lammas and Michaelmas Lands. These lands belonged to the freemen of the city, who gained revenue from them. Some of these lands where thrown open at certain times of the year, but no buildings were allowed to encroach on them. The city itself grew within its old walls, mainly by infilling in old gardens amongst its ancient timbered houses; buildings of brick with outside toilets and water pumps were erected around courtyards, known as the courts.

Spon Street and Spon End housed many watchmakers, and they looked for more space. In 1820 land was opened up for building at Poddy Croft, which is now gone, and Hertford Terrace, Hertford Square and Junction Street were built. Building activity continued in 1832 with the building of Thomas Street, Mill Street and Albion Street over the site of Crow Moat, an ancient moated house. The next area to open up was near the ancient Swanswell Pool. Land here which had formerly belonged to

Spon Street as it is today, showing original and reconstructed medieval and Tudor buildings.

SPON STREET 2004 C169763k (Paul Baron)

FORD STREET 2004 C169781k (Paul Baron)

the Sir Thomas White Charity estate was sold to the Corporation in 1843 for the building of Hales Street, White Street, Jesson Street, Norton Street and Ford Street.

This building work began to extend beyond the Swanswell Pool into an area anciently called Harnall and later known as Hillfields. A list of events recorded in 1849 tells us that 'in 1828 the fields lying between Swanswell-pool and Primrose Hill began to be converted into building land. The first house to be erected in Hill-Fields, or as it is now called, 'New-Town,' is situated in King William-street, a row of houses adjoining the field in Harnal-lane, having been reared a short time before. There are now 6,000 inhabitants in the districts.' In 1841 St Peter's Church was built; it was

Did you know?

Mary Ann Evans, better known as the famous novelist George Eliot, was educated in Coventry and later came to live here. Her first published work was in the Coventry Herald, owned by her friend Charles Bray. Bray and his wife Cara and their circle had a huge effect on the mind of Mary Ann; they encouraged her to write and opened her up to the world. She places the trial scene in 'Adam Bede' in St Mary's Hall, and her novel 'Middlemarch' is based on Coventry. Mary Ann Evans may have been born near Nuneaton, but George Eliot the writer was literally born in Coventry.

possible to stand in the churchyard and look down the hill across the Swanswell and see Coventry amid the three spires.

In 1845 an Act of Parliament opened up more St Thomas White Charity land for building at Chapelfields, an area that took its name from an ancient lepers' chapel and leper colony. In 1846 Craven Street, Duke Street, Lord Street and Mount Street were laid out on the fields, and building lots were sold. By 1851, seventy houses had been built - mainly for watchmakers. In 1852 building began to expand into the Earlsdon area when land between Elsdon Lane (Earlsdon Street) and Whor Lane (Beechwood Avenue) was laid out as eight streets with plots for self-building. This watchmakers' area continued to develop, especially after the opening of Albany Road in 1898 by the Duchess of Albany.

Watch making was a major trade in the city, beginning in the 18th century and reaching its peak in the 19th century, making Coventry one of the top watch manufacturing cities in England. Many watchmakers worked from home and were part of a chain, each supplying a watch part; few made entire watches. These parts were created by individuals and passed along until the final product was complete. There were many small workshops, and also factories, such as Rotherham & Sons in Spon Street.

In 1915 Arthur Walsgrove told the Coventry Herald of his life at Rotherham's from 1848 to 1911, a period spanning the watch trade's height to its decline: 'America had not begun to manufacture, and Coventry watch makers did a large trade with that country and the colonies ... It was after the Civil War ... that America began to seriously compete ... They turned their attention to the use of machinery which was really of English manufacture ... gradually they got the whole work into their hands. Coventry manufacturers always had the competition of the Swiss and did little business with the continent. When I was apprenticed the city was full of watchmakers, ... many having customers in all parts of the British Isles. Now they could be easily counted. It used to be the ambition of English people to wear English watches ... now ... Swiss cost less.'

Arthur recalled the old Coventry-made verge watch: 'The proper name was the vertical watch. Of course they have long gone out ... It was a very good watch for agricultural labourers and others engaged in dirty work. They did not keep such exact time that is expected of the modern watch, but they were very suitable for the class of people who bought them ... They were large and heavy, a 'good pocketful,' with a bold dial and double case. They would stand a good deal of knocking about.'

When the Franco-German War broke out in 1870, Arthur recalled that there was no trade being done across Europe, and people suddenly felt the need to own an English watch. The trade over the following year was huge, and the Coventry watchmakers, producing often handmade gold and silver watches, had difficulty meeting the demand. When asked what watchmakers did in their leisure time, Arthur replied: 'Some kept dogs, being fond of rabbit coursing, or they matched them to run races. Walking was a common form of recreation, Kenilworth, Bubbenhall and Berkswell Lane being popular resorts with some. Bubbenhall and Brinklow Wakes always attracted a number ... You would often see Coventry watchmakers in groups ... still wearing their long white aprons sauntering through the country lanes, some of them perhaps gathering flowers. Pigeon-keeping was a popular fancy ... Quite a lot of men were canary keepers ... In many top shops scores of canaries were kept.' Finally he added: 'The price of a good Coventry watch was £3, and it would last a lifetime.'

Kevitt Rotherham (of watch-making fame) said in 1923 that in the 1860s, when the weaving and watch industries slumped, it was the watchmakers who supplied the workforce for the newly created cycle manufacturing industry. The watchmakers, unlike the weavers, were used to working to minute measurements and to crafting in metal. It is generally believed that the first cycle was brought to Coventry from Paris by

Spon Street was the home of watch making, and it is home to the Coventry Watch Project.

SPON STREET 2004 C169707k (David McGrory)

COVENTRY WATCHES
ZZZ00395 (David McGrory Collection)

Coventry watches made by A H Read in the late 1890s.

Rowley Turner in 1868. However, a certain J Newark claimed that he built the first cycle in Bayley Lane from plans created by a smith, William Fardon of Stoneleigh. This all-metal, spoked-wheeled cycle with India-rubber tyres was ridden by him around Coventry for six months before it was sold to a Parisian chef, who is thought to have taken it to France.

The story of the origin of the cycle trade in Coventry is inextricably linked to a Sussex-born farm boy, James Starley, who came to Coventry in the hot summer of 1861 during the collapse of the weaving trade and the slump in the watch trade. Starley, with Josiah Turner and others, set up the Coventry Machinist Company producing Starley's improved sewing machines. After Rowley Turner, the company's agent, brought the French Michaux cycle to Coventry, Starley studied it and improved it, and the Machinist Company built its first Coventry-made cycle, and called it the Coventry Model.

In 1870 Starley and Hillman left the company. They set up in St John's Street and produced the Aerial, the first all-metal framed, geared penny-farthing. This particular cycle became so common that it acquired the name the Ordinary. The partnership with Hillman did not last. Starley became partners with Borthwick Smith, and started the Aerial Works in St Agnes Lane. (It is appropriate that the present transport museum stands on its site). During these years Starley went on to invent most of the things found on the modern cycle, and even some on the motor car, such as the differential gear: he first created this for a four-wheeler called the Convertible Sociable.

In 1891 one writer wrote of the old boneshakers, saying: 'It was Mr Starley again who improved upon these unwieldy machines, that they eventually became saleable articles. The present writer was one of the first to ride one of these antiquated and awe inspiring constructions, on its importation from France, and well does he remember the delight, when after many painful journeys on the horrible wooden instrument, he had the satisfaction of seeing it being smashed to atoms by a butcher's cart and eventually replaced by one of Mr Starley's Aerials!'

Starley set the wheels in motion for the production of cycles in Coventry, making it a world centre for the trade. It is not surprising that he gained the title 'Father of the Cycle', and three years after his death in 1881 a monument was erected to his memory.

> # Did you know?
>
> On 15 December 1857 Charles Dickens read his 'Christmas Carol' in Coventry's Corn Exchange in Hertford Street. He came again on 4 December 1858 and dined with 70 gentlemen at the Castle Hotel, where he was presented with a Coventry-made Rotherham's watch. He afterwards visited St Mary's Hall and Rotherham's, and promised he would wear his Coventry watch forever, which is exactly what he did.

James Starley's sons continued the business in St John's Street after his death. 'Big Bill' Starley, who himself brought out 138 patents, pushed the company to expand, and soon its reputation spread across the globe; Starley's opened a second factory in Paris. The next great step in the evolution of the cycle was the creation of the safety cycle by Harry Lawson, who will reappear with the birth of the motorcar. Lawson's design did not take off, however. It was John Kemp Starley, the nephew of James, who in 1884 created the most popular safety cycle, called the Rover, on which all modern cycles are based. The demand for the Rover was so great that many other cycle manufacturers copied the design;

The Broadgate Clock

THE BROADGATE CLOCK AND BELL c1955
C16901 1a

When the clock was first constructed it was given an electric motor. This proved unreliable, and it was replaced with the mechanism from the original market clock made in 1870 by an ex-Rotherham's employee, Edward Thomas Loseby. He was so confident in his skill that he promised to pay £1 for every second the clock lost. Needless to say, the clock was so reliable that Loseby did not have to pay anything. The clock ran without a hitch until 1942, when it was removed and the market tower demolished. Loseby's mechanism now runs the Broadgate Clock; every hour is stuck upon no ordinary bell, but the old bell which struck the hour in the old market bell tower from 1867.

Coventry's cycle trade boomed, with Rover, Rudge and Humber, to name a few, among the manufacturers. In 1897 one firm alone in Coventry was producing 40,000 cycles a year. The trade continued to thrive, but gradually during the 20th century the motorcar became dominant, and the cycle trade disappeared.

Coventry's staple industry from medieval times was weaving, and during the 18th century the art of weaving silk ribbons had flourished in the city. In 1820 the introduction of the Jacquard loom made it easier and faster to produce decorative ribbons in large quantities. Amongst a population of 21,000 in 1821 there were 5,000 silk workers. In 40 years the population had doubled, and so had the number working in silk. Originally all looms were hand-powered, but in 1831 Josiah Beck introduced the first steam looms into the city. The riot which ensued because of this led to the burning of his factory in Beck's Yard, off New Buildings.

It is hardly surprising that this violent incident (in which Beck himself suffered physical abuse by the mob) delayed the re-introduction of the steam-powered loom into the city for another six years. But eventually it returned, and by 1860 there were 2,500 steam looms in the city. Two unusual weaving factories in Coventry were Cash's purpose-built cottage factory by the canal, and Eli Green's triangle in Hillfields, a triangle of 67 houses with top shops, its looms powered by a single steam engine. Many weavers still worked from home, and five working handlooms could still be found in operation in Foleshill in 1927.

Problems with the trade began late in 1859, when factory weavers demanded to be paid by piecework and not by a fixed weekly wage. This resulted in a mass lockout, which lasted for eight weeks, when the Corporation intervened, fearing damage to the city's prosperity. Some mill owners capitulated, and many weavers returned to work, but some owners held out by employing blacklegs. This resulted in attacks on factories: one attack was launched by a mob numbering up to 3,000. It is not surprising that these owners soon gave in, and all the weavers returned to work.

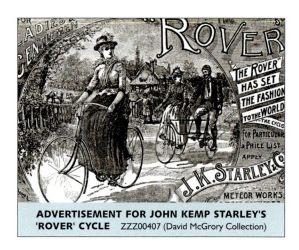

ADVERTISEMENT FOR JOHN KEMP STARLEY'S 'ROVER' CYCLE ZZZ00407 (David McGrory Collection)

There had been developments behind the scenes during the strike, and in February 1860 Gladstone, then Chancellor of the Exchequer, announced that the government had made a commercial treaty with France. Part of this treaty meant that the duty on French ribbons would be dropped. This caused a panic in Coventry, and a deputation was sent to London, but it was unsuccessful. When the act came into effect, the country was flooded with cheap French ribbons, which hit the Coventry trade. This was followed by America putting a high duty upon imported English ribbons. The Coventry trade quickly went into decline; then ribbons fell from fashion, and the trade collapsed. Employers tried to reduce the weavers' wages, which led to another strike.

The 19th Century

THE COURTYARD, ST MARY'S HALL 1892 30930

Here unemployed weavers queued to collect soup and bread made in the hall's medieval kitchen, the oldest in England. Also hundreds of weavers crushed together in the hall to hear a talk on emigration; over 4,000 eventually left the

THE CRIMEAN WAR CANNON 1892 30913

EARLY MOTOR CARS 1897 ZZZ00405 (David McGrory Collection)

These are the first GHCC vehicles, photographed in June/July 1897 soon after their completion. On the left sits Francis Baron, the works manager, at the tiller, and J H Barrows, the chief cashier. In the vehicle on the right are W McNeil, the wages clerk, at the tiller, and Baron's assistant, Davies, along with his fellow Great Horseless Carriage Company colleagues.

Coventry's silk weavers soon found themselves in trouble, and many took to raiding crops from the fields to save their families from starvation; some weavers did actually starve to death. Soup kitchens were opened, and Lord Leigh started an appeal fund - in 1862, 14,000 weavers were dependent on it. In the end, many who would have returned to work could not do so, because the work no longer existed. Around 4,000 emigrated, and only a couple of firms survived. One of these was Thomas Stevens, who began to weave book marks and silk pictures (Stevengraphs) which are still highly collectable. Weaving did survive into the 20th century in a limited way with the introduction of other types of weaving, such as worsted and coach lace.

The foundation of the British motor industry was laid in London in 1896 when the inventor of the safety cycle, Harry Lawson, chaired the first meeting of the British Motor Syndicate. Knowing that Coventry was a pool of labour, Lawson set up a factory at an old cotton mill in Draper's Field, Radford. In May 1896 he started

The Crimean War Cannons

THE CRIMEAN WAR CANNON 1892 30913x

The Royal Field Artillery captured two siege cannons (dating from 1799) from the Crimean War. The two Russian guns were brought back to the city in July 1858 as a gift from the famed Lord Cardigan, and were first kept in Coventry Barracks. Later the guns were moved: one was placed on Greyfriars Green, the other in Swanswell Park. The Greyfriars Green gun remained a landmark until its carriage was smashed by a string of bombs in 1940. It lay under a tree until it was taken away and scrapped for the war effort in 1943.

Did you know?

Dame Ellen Terry, England's most famous Victorian actress, was born at 5 Market Street, Coventry on 27 February 1847 while her parents were on tour. Another famous actress connected to the city is England's greatest 18th-century actress, Sarah Siddons. She was married at Holy Trinity Church.

the Great Horseless Carriage Company at the mill, which was shared with Daimler and other companies. The mill, known as Motor Mills, was claimed to be the birthplace of the first British-built motor car. While Daimler initially built engines, the GHCC produced British versions of the Boulee tricar. Francis Baron, works manager of the company, later said that the company built its own design of vehicle with a Daimler engine; one of these was supplied to Lord Iveagh for the Duke of York. Baron says that this vehicle was finished in June 1897, almost two months before the first Daimler-built car was completed, whose proving run took place in October. In 1935 Baron wrote of the first car in the 'Autocar' magazine: 'I contend that the car I have mentioned, which worked continuously without the slightest hitch, being the first petrol car built in England, contributed as much to the present motor industry as George Stephenson's first locomotive to railway development.'

From these early beginnings the British motor industry was born at a Coventry cotton mill. Many cycle manufacturers such as Swift, Singer, Riley, Rover and Humber, to name but a few, turned from cycle to motorcar production.

In 1968, Thomas Kimberley recorded his impressions of Coventry as he remembered it during the last years of the 19th century: 'Coventry was a garrison town with varied industrial and commercial interests [weaving, watch making and cycle manufacturing] … Agriculture, too should not be forgotten, there was a Corn Exchange … [and] coal was mined on the fringes of the city, notably Binley … and Wyken. A quiet town, its population in general law-abiding and with few exceptions friendly, cheerful and hard working; a close knit community … By today's standards … conditions were severe for the artisan class, most of whom rose early and worked long hours … Streets were safe, children playing therein with little risk from horse drawn vehicles, herds of cattle, flocks of sheep the only other users of the public highway … Lighting of streets, alleys and courts was by gas … Public houses had no strict closing times and rum and coffee at 6.00am on the way to work was not uncommon. The use of a clay pipe for smoking was general, many of which were made locally … [and] chewing tobacco was common, also snuff taking.'

The status of City and County of Coventry, which was given to the city by Henry VI, was lost in 1842 after residents in the suburbs brought an action against the city over being charged high rates, the same as the city itself, but not getting the benefits the city enjoyed. The case was won, and the County of Coventry came to an end. After this, the city limits were redefined, and the enclosure of parts of the freemen's Lammas and Michaelmas Lands helped the city to spread. In 1890 the villages of Earlsdon, Radford and the Red Lane district were taken into the city bounds, followed in 1899 by Stoke and Foleshill. Coventry had begun to grow more and more as new people came to the city looking to work in its growing industries.

COVENTRY – *a history and celebration of the city*

COVENTRY, GREYFRIARS GREEN 1892 30921

This area along Warwick Row and down to Stoneleigh Terrace was once used by the local cavalry regiments for practice. For a time in the 19th century it was also home to Coventry Fair. The statue of the benefactor Sir Thomas White was erected in 1882 on the site of an old pool called the Red Sea. In the 15th century this was also home to the ducking stool.

ORDNANCE SURVEY MAP 1887

The 19th Century 83

CHAPTER FOUR

The 20th Century

A E W MASON, the author of 'The Four Feathers' and MP for Coventry, wrote at the beginning of the century: 'It is a city where a few steps will take you out of the thronged streets into some quiet old garden with the peace of antique memories: some old close of plaster and black beams: some old room with windows deep-set in four foot walls, and wide hearths of centuries ago. And round about these old places stands a ring of factories, where in good times, the lights blaze until the morning, and the whir of its machines never ceases in your ears.'

Coventry was really like this into the 20th century: hundreds of ancient timbered houses were interspersed by factories. J H Wade wrote in 1932: 'Coventry is now a city of 175,000 inhabitants, and in spite of the expansion of its industrial suburbs, retains some remnants of its earlier rural surroundings. The approach from Kenilworth is still finely timbered … The ancient heart of Coventry is intricate, and some of its streets are narrow, but this adds considerably to its quaintness and interest, for in these byways are a large number of old houses. It is not an easy place to find one's way about in … Coventry is difficult to envisage as a whole but a striking and characteristic view of it can be secured from Greyfriars Green, once the scene of the city's fair, where the three tapering spires are seen rising gracefully above the wilderness of buildings.'

HAY LANE 2004 C169732k (Paul Baron)

A typical old Coventry street containing a mix of ancient buildings.

From the start of the century the population had risen considerably; in 1901-2 there was an influx of workers from Wales, Scotland and Ireland. In 1901 it was 69,978, and ten years later this had risen hugely to 106,377. Industries continued to draw people to the city, and the population peaked in 1966 with 335,238. To accommodate the growing population, more houses were needed, and many were built by private builders. The council built its first houses in the city in Short Street and Narrow Lane (Kingfield Road) in 1908. More were added in 1914-15, and were followed in 1925 by a major municipal housing project in Radford on former Michaelmas and Lammas land. By 1945 nearly 20,000 houses had been built around the city's suburbs. Municipal building continued into the 1970s, but most modern housing, such as the Daimler Green Estate built on the site of the Daimler factory and aerodrome, was constructed by private companies.

The expanding population meant that the ancient schools of Bablake and Henry VIII had to expand, and new schools were built in the growing areas of the city. Some grew around the former homes of industrialists, such as Coundon Court, once the home of George Singer of Singer Cycles, and Barr's Hill, the former home of John Kemp Starley of cycle fame. Lancaster College, which

COVENTRY UNIVERSITY 2004 ZZZ01585 (CVOne)

This is 'the castle,' home to Coventry University's library.

opened in the city in 1960, became the Coventry Polytechnic and more recently Coventry University. It continues to expand in the city centre, using many older buildings such as the former Morris works and the old Coliseum building. It also has a huge purpose-built library using modern forms of energy conservation; its unusual shape and high ventilation turrets have earned it the nickname of 'the castle'. Another university is the strangely named University of Warwick, which stands in the Canley district of Coventry. It currently has around 16,000 students and has an international reputation, taking students from all over the world. The huge campus has been built on former farmland; it is home to one of the country's best arts centres, which boasts some 233,000 visitors a year.

Coventry's cycle industry continued into the 20th century, along with the production of motorbikes by companies like Rudge and Triumph. From the First World War, Coventry also developed a notable aircraft industry. Humber built early monoplanes such as the Lovelace and the Bleriot, and Daimler at Radford built BE12 fighters for the Royal Flying Corps. Other companies, such as Standard, came into their own with wartime production of numerous aircraft, especially the famed Mosquito fighter-bomber.

However, the most notable company, not only locally but nationally, was Armstrong Whitworth Aircraft, which was formed at Whitley Abbey Aerodrome in 1920. Here they built the first standard RAF fighter, the Siskin, followed by the Atlas biplane and the Argosy Mark II - the company's first passenger airliner. In March 1936 the first Whitley bomber flew from Whitley, and later with the outbreak of war became the first English bomber to penetrate German airspace. The Whitley became the workhorse of the RAF, and by the end of the war 1,812 bombers had been built at the Whitley and Baginton works. It is surprising that not a single one survives. During the war years, AWA also built other bombers, including the Lancaster and the Wellington, and in 1946 the company produced the AW52, the first all-metal flying wing, which was 50 years ahead of its time.

Did you know?

In 1907 Frank Whittle, the inventor of the jet engine, was born in Newcome Road, Earlsdon. In Millennium Place a huge sculpture called the Whittle Arch commemorates Coventry's world-changing son.

Coventry also became notable for its many engineering firms, such as Alfred Herbert, the largest machine tool factory in the world, and also Coventry Gauge & Tool and Matrix. In 1972 it was recorded that 200,000 people worked in Coventry, with 68,000 in the motor industry, 45,000 in electrical and general engineering, 15,000 in professional work, 13,000 in distribution, 7,000 in administration, 7,000 in construction and 6,000 in textiles.

JAGUARS AT THE COVENTRY TRANSPORT MUSEUM ZZZ01587

The motor industry was, however, the greatest draw to those who were looking for a new beginning. Coventry became 'motor city', where the well-paid car worker had the highest car ownership in the land. One of the city's most noted firms is Jaguar; the company began in 1928 as the Swallow Sidecar & Coach Building Company, known as SS Cars, in the old White & Poppe munitions factory in Whitmore Park. Under the direction of its founder, William Lyons, the company produced such classics as the SS100. Because of the war and the implications of the letters SS, the company changed its name to Jaguar Cars, and continued to produce high quality vehicles such as the Mark II and the E-Type series. In 1952 Lyons was unable to expand on his site, so he moved all production to their old wartime shadow factory in Browns Lane. Here, Jaguar continued until recently to produce one of the finest marques in the world.

Another Coventry great was the Standard Motor Company, started by Reginald Maudsley in Much Park Street in 1903. Here he built his first car, the 6hp Motor Victoria. He soon established a bigger works at Bishopgate Green, and there built the first car to carry the Standard name; it was followed in 1913 by their first mass-produced vehicle, the Standard Model S. During the First World War the company began producing aircraft and munitions, and opened new factories in Cash's Lane and Canley. In 1921 car production was back to normal, and the company released its new tourer, the Model SLO. In the 1930s its Flying Standard range was extremely popular and affordable. During the Second World

War the company produced huge numbers of aeroplanes, including the famed Mosquito fighter-bombers. Later, in peacetime, it released the first Vanguard, perhaps its most popular car. In 1953 the Basic Eight was released: advertised as the world's cheapest car, and costing £399, it became known as the 'People's Car'. This was followed in 1954 with the popular Standard Ten, and then the following year by the handsome Vanguard III. Standard Cars were extremely popular, and although Standard were one of the smaller manufacturers, they took a good section of the market. Their last car, the Standard Ensign, rolled off the Canley production line in May 1963. Jaguar and Standard are but two of a long list of Coventry motor manufacturers; others include Daimler, Humber, Riley, Lancaster, Swift and Alvis.

Through the First and Second World Wars, Coventry manufacturers changed to war work, supplying weapons and equipment for land, air and sea. This meant that during the Second World War shadow factories were erected in open countryside outside the city, and thousands of war workers came to the city. Coventry's war production was an important factor in this country's survival, but it also made the city a target. The first raid in the area was on 25 June 1940, when bombs

Broadgate photographed after the big raid. Note the clock stopped at 10.40pm, and smoke still drifting past the tower and spire of Holy Trinity Church.

BROADGATE 1940   ZZZ00404 (David McGrory Collection)

were dropped on nearby Ansty Aerodrome and local villages. The first heavy raid on Coventry took place on 25 August when the Rex Cinema was destroyed; how ironic that on the following day it was to show 'Gone with the Wind'.

The most notorious raid on the city took place on the night of 14/15 November 1940, when around 500 German bombers left France in droves and bombed the city centre for 11 long hours. Alec Clemson, an Auxiliary Fire Officer who later moved to Australia, wrote of the event: 'As I cycled down Daventry Road hill flares lit up the sky and the glow growing over the city turned to orange ... John Mileson, Station Officer, called out 'You've missed the Whitley crew Alec, they've gone to Broadgate.' I pedalled towards the glare of the city. Little Park Street leading to the Council House was deserted. Leaving my cycle by the Midland Bank I ran past Anslow's, the furnishers and along High Street to Broadgate. There was an engine and turntable ladder up at Lloyd's Bank roof. In the town centre ... there was ... activity wherever I looked. There was the crackling of burning wood and the shock of explosions in that ring of fire. Broadgate was aflame and I searched desperately for the crew with whom I trained ... Owen Owen's store was ablaze and in the glow of sparks made by falling structures in Ironmonger Row, a fireman went down. He hung onto the branch-pipe, which thrashed him from side to side, until I reached him and grabbed it ... A voice, fireman Kimberley's I believe, called urgently, 'Come out of that - the next floor is caving in.'

Broadgate as it looks today from Trinity churchyard.

BROADGATE 2004 C169708k (David McGrory)

'I turned back to Broadgate, it was just then that the next floor did cave in and belched out through the doorway. Bombs were falling and the explosions followed. Their whine could be heard momentarily drowning the roar of flames and the hiss of water as it turned to steam. As I reached Boots there was a nearer whine of a bomb, I leaned for shelter against a car. The hit was made in Market Street, just off Broadgate. The car rocked on its springs. Incendiary bombs were still bursting into flower here and there, neatly planted rows of them along the road, ignored by firemen energetically concerned with burning buildings. Moving nearer to Smithford Street, I fell in with the

Here we see the cathedral ruins after they had been cleared.

THE CATHEDRAL c1955 C169012

Coniston Road crew ... I joined the lone man doing his best to hold the branch-pipe steady. The two of us managed it well enough but the heat was terrific. As I looked back to Boots the car by which I had stood burst into flames ... There was a thin scream in the air and a red blinding blast, Astley's took another salvo. The front of the ground floor shop coughed out at us and the stench of burning paint nearly made me retch. The fireman I was helping, Edgar Humphries, was knocked to his knees by the blast. He gasped 'Can you hold it?' As I answered him through the smoke and fumes he staggered away to the pump ... The water was failing and soon there was none.

'Frenzied activity took place to try to relay water from the Sherbourne ... but the distance was too great ... Crews began to leave Broadgate. Someone said that hundreds had been drowned in the Co-op shelters when the mains burst. Others told us that the explosions just off Broadgate had destroyed the cathedral. We cursed the bastards overhead! Broadgate was still a ring of fire while above, the drone of the planes still registered in our awareness. My face was red and sore from the heat and the whole shopping area was on fire ... The fire crews had deserted Broadgate and only several unattached men, as I was, were left trying to stem the lesser fires ... It was 1am and there seemed little one could do so I decided to see how my family had fared.'

Bombs continued to fall all night. The cathedral was destroyed by incendiary bombs, and the centre of Coventry was devastated. Finally at 6.15am on the following morning the raid stopped and the All Clear sounded. People slowly emerged from the shelters into the flaming, smoking city; in it lay 554 dead and 865 injured. Overnight most major buildings had sustained some damage, 4,330 homes had been destroyed and thousands damaged, and 75 per cent of the city's industry had received some damage. The world was shocked at the devastation wrought on Coventry that night, and all-out relief was given to the city to restore mains electricity, gas and other services. Many factories were back in production in days, and full production returned within several weeks. The resilience of Coventry's people shone through the destruction, and that year

BROADGATE c1955 C169023

Christmas was celebrated as it always was. Some, however, could not be there.

Coventry endured 41 raids altogether; other particularly heavy ones took place in April 1941. The last bomber flew over the city in August 1942. By the end of this period, 1,236 had died in the bombing, and 808 received a mass burial in London Road Cemetery. Others, such as war workers who came from elsewhere, were taken home for burial by their families. Others were never found.

The Golden Elephant

BROADGATE c1955 C169023a

The golden elephant was the first thing erected here in the new precinct. It was made by Motor Panels, and served the dual purpose of marking the top of the precinct and the site of the Savings for Reconstruction Exhibition.

No sooner had the rubble been cleared than plans were under way to rebuild the city. Plans had already been made before the war to rebuild under the city's first architect Donald Gibson. In February 1941 both Gibson and City Engineer Ernest Ford put forward plans for the rebuilding of the central area. Gibson's plan was accepted, and in May 1948 a new island Broadgate was officially opened by Princess Elizabeth. In 1949 the famous Lady Godiva statue was added, to be followed by Broadgate House in 1953.

BROADGATE c1965 C169022

COVENTRY, BROADGATE c1965 C169022

The 20th Century 97

Owen Owen's store overlooks Broadgate Island. It is interesting that one of the oldest things found in Coventry was discovered between the lamp post on the left and the bronze statue of Godiva: an older piece of bronze, a bronze axe-head dating to around 650BC.

THE LADY GODIVA STATUE ZZZ00403

Sir William Reid Dick's famous statue of Lady Godiva stands on Broadgate Island.

who has laid very soundly the foundations of the new Coventry.' Ling's first design was a new railway station, because he had noted its appalling state when he first came to the city; it had, of course, suffered in the bombing during the war. He then redesigned the Lower Precinct and added Smithford Way. He also added Mercia House to give height and the Locarno, now the Central Library, and the Belgrade Theatre for entertainment. These years of rebuilding were symbolised by the phoenix rising from the ashes, and this emblem became a supporter on the Coventry coat of arms in 1959.

MERCIA HOUSE 2004 C169761k (Paul Baron)

This was followed by the Upper Precinct, built in what later became known as Festival of Britain style; it had two tiers - the idea came from the famous Rows in Chester. The new Owen Owen building, now Allders, opened in October 1954, and it was followed by the completion of the Upper Precinct in 1955. Gibson left the city in 1955 and was replaced by Arthur Ling, who said: 'I think that a lot of good ideas and planning that have now become accepted by other authorities were pioneered in Coventry, and I am very conscious that I am following a man

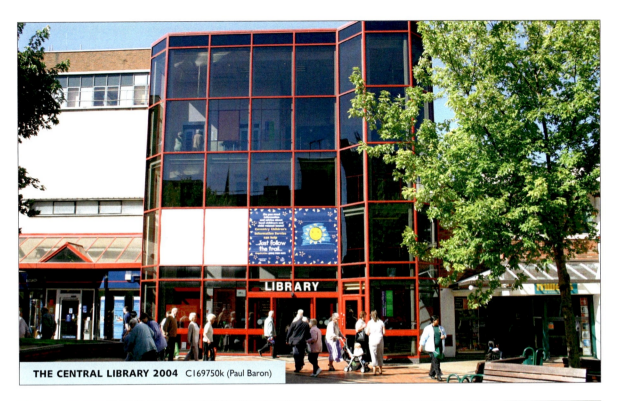
THE CENTRAL LIBRARY 2004 C169750k (Paul Baron)

BELGRADE THEATRE 2004 C169759k (Paul Baron)

ALDERS DEPARTMENT STORE, BROADGATE 2004 C169746k (Paul Baron)

THE PRECINCT c1965 C169020

We are looking across the upper precinct towards British Home Stores and the original Woolworth building, which ran along Market Way to the corner of the Lower Precinct. When the site was dug up for the building of Woolworth's, ancient finds came to light: hundreds of oak piles were found driven into the bed of the Bablake, which stretched around here.

The second great rebuilding scheme in the city was the new cathedral designed by Basil Spence, who would later receive a knighthood for his work. Spence said that when he visited the ruins of St Michael's, he looked through one of the north windows and saw a vision of the new cathedral growing out of the old. He saw the massive glass front and the tapestry behind the altar, and within 24 hours his first design was created. The 270ft-long, 80ft-wide building houses the work of the best artists of the 20th century. Graham Sutherland's massive tapestry shows Christ in glory surrounded by the emblems of the four evangelists; the wonderful baptistery window was designed by John Piper and made by Patrick Reyntiens; and the fantastic glass south wall covered in angels and saints engraved on the glass was created by John Hutton, whose ashes rest at the base of this, probably his greatest work.

The new cathedral of St Michael cost £1,385,000 and was dedicated by Her Majesty the Queen in May 1962. Millions of visitors have been to the cathedral, which despite now being over 40 years old was voted one of Britain's best-loved buildings in 1999. The cathedral is not just a place of ministry and a tourist attraction; it is also the centre of the Ministry of International Reconciliation, which was formed after the destruction of the old cathedral. The ministry is active throughout the world in bringing, and trying to bring, peace and reconciliation to those in need.

The New Cathedral

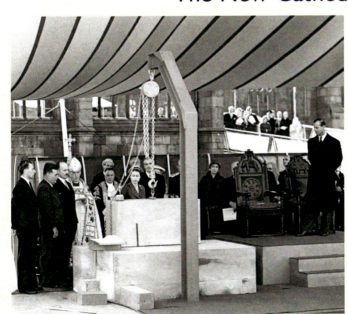

The Queen lays the foundation stone of the new Cathedral of St Michael on 22 March 1956. Altogether 34,000 stones weighing between 1 cwt and 1 ton were used in the building. The roof was covered with 29,000 feet of copper, and the floor with 27,000 feet of marble.

THE CATHEDRAL, THE QUEEN LAYS THE FOUNDATION STONE
1956 ZZZ00400 (David McGrory Collection)

COVENTRY CATHEDRAL c1965 C169076

COVENTRY CATHEDRAL c1965 C169076

EPSTEIN'S ST MICHAEL AND THE DEVIL
ZZZ00402 (David McGrory)

Sir Jacob Epstein's 19ft 6in, 4-ton bronze statue of St Michael defeating the devil is considered one of his last great works.

Coventry's third great work of construction of the 20th century was its ring road, which surrounds 450 acres of the city centre. This road, carried for much of its way on concrete legs, has kept the centre of Coventry relatively free from traffic congestion since its completion. There are, however, some plans in the near future to lower the section running from the Foleshill Road to the Swanswell to help improve the look of the area. Broadgate, the city's heart and the entrance to Coventry Castle, was from 1948 an island untouched by

Did you know?

Coventry was the birthplace of Ska music in the 1980s with bands such as The Specials and The Selector.

The 20th Century

THE SKYDOME COMPLEX, SPON STREET 2004 ZZZ01582 (CVOne)

The SkyDome complex stands at the bottom of Spon Street.

WEST ORCHARDS 77701589 (Coventry Evening Telegraph)

The glass dome in West Orchards is said to be the largest in Europe.

pedestrians and home only to the Lady Godiva statue, flowers and grass. It was pedestrianised in the 1970s, and in 1990 half of it was built upon with the Cathedral Lanes Shopping Centre.

More building work took place in 1997 with the demolition of part of 1950s Smithford Way and the creation of the £50 million West Orchards Shopping Centre with its huge glass typanteum, said to be the largest in Europe. The next building was on the site of the old Rudge/GEC factory in Spon Street. This was demolished and in October 1999, the £33 million SkyDome complex was opened on the site, home to a number of themed bars, a cinema and a stadium, which is used for small concerts, basketball and ice hockey. However, it was not just modern architecture that went up: back in the 1970s,

Spon Street was enhanced by the rebuilding of old Coventry timbered buildings amongst those which already existed there. These dated from the 14th to the 17th centuries.

Coventry's canal basin was also restored, and new buildings, designed to be in keeping, were added. Outside the city centre, business parks were developed, along with major retail parks such as the Alvis Retail Park, Gallagher Retail Park and Central Six, and other parks such as the University of Warwick Science Park and the Binley Business Park. One of the largest urban regeneration schemes in Europe is the Coventry Business Park in Canley, which not only houses internationally-known companies, but also a large Sainsbury's store. In the last year of the 20th century over £150 million was being spent on new developments in Coventry.

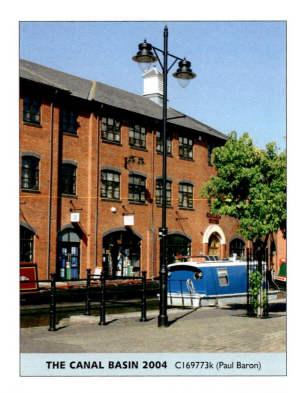

THE CANAL BASIN 2004 C169773k (Paul Baron)

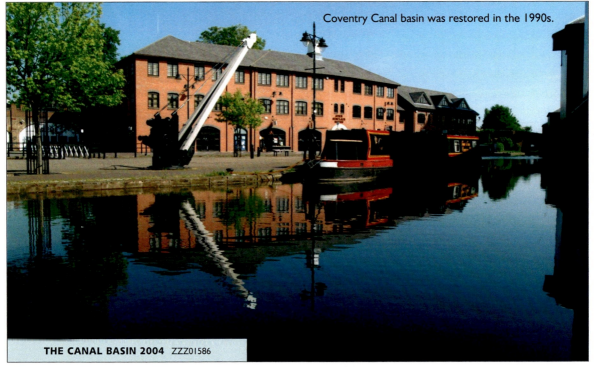

Coventry Canal basin was restored in the 1990s.

THE CANAL BASIN 2004 ZZZ01586

The 20th Century

THE CANAL BASIN 2004 C169772k (Paul Baron)

THE STATUE OF JAMES BRINDLEY, THE CANAL BASIN 2004 C169774K (Paul Baron)

> ### Did you know?
> In 1987 Coventry City Football Club won the FA Cup for the only time in their history.

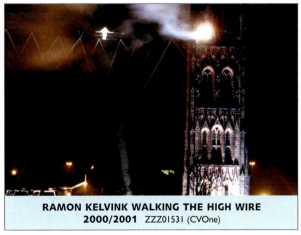

RAMON KELVINK WALKING THE HIGH WIRE 2000/2001 ZZZ01531 (CVOne)

As the 20th century gave way to the 21st, the French high wire walker Ramon Kelvink walked the high wire between Holy Trinity Church and St Michael's.

BUTCHER ROW 1892 C169001

COVENTRY, HIGH STREET AND BROADGATE c1955 C169003p

CHAPTER FIVE

Now and the Future

COVENTRY – *a history and celebration of the city*

THE PATTERN of Coventry's history has been one of slumps and rebuilding, from trade, from bombs, from the economy. But Coventry always strives, wins, and rebuilds; that is why the phoenix, symbol of resurrection, is so appropriate for the city. Few cities can boast the great history that Coventry has, and few have gone through the massive changes it has seen, the results of bulldozers and bombs. Few others can show the great developments Coventry has made as it set the mark for others with futuristic developments such as the pedestrian precinct, an idea copied throughout the world. Coventry is innovative, and not afraid to face the future.

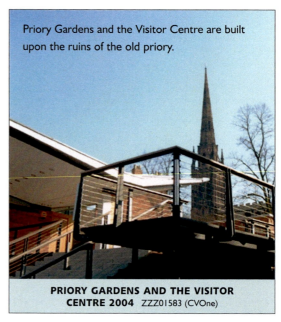

Priory Gardens and the Visitor Centre are built upon the ruins of the old priory.

PRIORY GARDENS AND THE VISITOR CENTRE 2004 ZZZ01583 (CVOne)

THE PRECINCT 2004 C169709k (David McGrory)

Looking from the Upper to Lower Precinct today.

Now and the Future

THE TRANSPORT MUSEUM 2004 C169777k (Paul Baron)

THE TRANSPORT MUSEUM. SHOWING THE TIME ZONE CLOCK 2004 C169778K (Paul Baron)

The beginning of the 21st century in Coventry saw very many developments. One of these was the completion of the Phoenix Initiative, which began with one of the most important archeological excavations in the country and ended with a new tourist attraction - the Priory Visitor Centre, with a medieval undercroft exhibited under the new cathedral offices. The initiative also provided a number of flats and loft-style executive apartments leading down the hillside to the huge Whittle Arches and into Millennium Place; it also provided the new re-fronted Coventry Transport Museum, which houses one of the largest transport collections in the world, including the two fastest cars in the world. To the amazement of many visitors to the city, entrance is free.

> **Did you know?**
>
> The excavation of Coventry Priory was considered one of the most important archeological digs in the country, and the only dig to feature twice in the 'Time Team' TV programme.

From Millennium Place, which has already been used for concerts, a glass bridge curves over the remaining section of the city wall, and over Lady Herbert's Garden, to come to ground in a modern garden beyond. Things are to change here in the future: there is talk of dropping the ring road to ground level, and opening up the prospect towards Swanswell Pool. Coventry's Lower Precinct has recently been transformed (with the help of £38 million) from a windy and uninspiring corner into a clean modern shopping area covered by a glass canopy housing new shops and restaurants, with a new arcade leading to the refurbished market. This was done without losing the original feel of Ling's design. The Bull Ring and Shelton Square have also been improved, and so has the precinct itself, which has new lights and paving and a new public fountain. Over the last four years, numbers of high quality housing projects with stylish apartments have taken place in the city centre, and on the outskirts huge housing projects have taken place, such as Daimler Green and

> **Did you know?**
>
> Coventry is one of the few places in the country with a special lighting scheme on its larger buildings. They are programmed to respond to varying temperatures, which means that at night when the temperature drops the lights turn blue.

MILLENNIUM PLACE AT NIGHT 2004 ZZZ01581 (CVOne)

Now and the Future

Electric Wharf, both in Radford, which have reused industrial land.

New building work goes on apace in the suburbs with the conversion of the old Keresley Colliery and Home Fire Plant into the Prologis Business Park. Nearby the new Jaguar Arena is under construction, which will be the new home of Coventry City Football Club and an arena for events such as concerts. Next to this will stand the largest Tesco store in Europe, an 8,000-seater exhibition hall, and a casino. At Bell Green and Willenhall there are plans for the complete rebuilding of the shopping areas and some housing, while at Walsgrave a new large hospital is under construction. Coventry Airport has gained a new terminal, and cheap air flights can now be made from here across Europe. Back in the city centre, the Belgrade Theatre is to be upgraded, and on the land behind Bond Street a whole new complex of housing and shops called Belgrade Plaza is to be developed. The arts will also benefit from the rebuilding work at the Herbert: an extension will house media studios, and there are future plans for the housing of both archives and local studies together, overlooking the newly-completed square between the cathedral and Coventry University. In total more than £1 billion is being spent on building programmes, which are the biggest since after the war.

Coventry is a thriving city, much visited and appreciated by tourists the world over. It is a

> ### Did you know?
>
> *Each year over 5 million people visit Coventry and contribute around £173 million to the local economy.*

city which never stands still; it is constantly developing, gaining national awards for its architecture, and even winning Britain in Bloom awards. It is a city of surprises, from its modern architecture to its historic gems such as St Mary's Hall. It is also now a thriving multicultural city, giving a home to people the world over. It is a city full of life, with its jazz festival and its yearly Godiva Festival, which begins with a Godiva ride and ends with one of the largest music festivals in the Midlands held in the Memorial Park.

Coventry, like the phoenix, rose from the ashes; and as it enters the 21st century, the phoenix still burns brighter than ever.

THE LOWER PRECINCT 2004 ZZZ01584 (CVOne)

Ling's Lower Precinct has been modernised and thrives today.

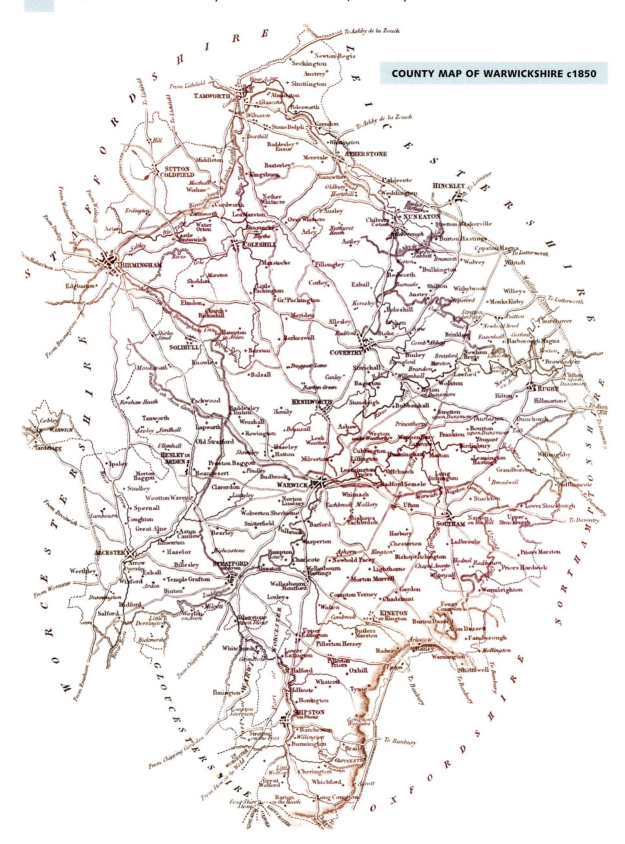

COUNTY MAP OF WARWICKSHIRE c1850

ACKNOWLEDGEMENTS

For photographs I would like to acknowledge Peter Walters and CVOne and Andrew Patterson who took their photographs. Holy Trinity Church for the Doom Painting photograph. Coventry City Libraries, Local Studies, Coventry Evening Telegraph and the Coventry Transport Museum. Paul Baron from Frith Books, also Heather Head, John Ashby, Trevor Pring, Craig Taylor. Neil Crowley for his line drawing and David Morgan for an engraving. The rest of the photos and illustrations were either taken by myself or from the David McGrory Collection.

BIBLIOGRAPHY

Burbidge, F B Old Coventy & Lady Godiva, Birmingham, 1952.
Clemson, Alec Written memories, Australia, 1985.
Coventry Evening Telegraph, Cuttings.
Coventry Herald, various editions, Coventry City Libraries, Local Studies.
Coventry Mercury, as above.
Coventry Standard, as above.
Coss, P R Early Records of Medieval Coventry.
Dugdale, W The Antiquities of Coventre, Coventry, 1765.
Harris, M D Catalogue of the Trinity Deeds, Herald, 1913-14.
Harris, M D The Coventry Leet Book, Early English Text Society, 1907-13.
McGrory, David A History of Coventry, Phillimore, 2003.
McGrory, David An Illustrated Guide to Coventry's Suburbs, Breedon, 2003.
McGrory, David The City of Coventry: Images form the Past, Jones/Sands, 1996.
Poole, B Coventry: It's History & Antiquities, Coventry, 1869.
Searby, Peter Coventry in Crisis, Coventry Historical Association booklet, 1977.
Sharp, Thomas History and Antiquities of the City of Coventry, William Fretton edition, 1871.
Whitley, T W The Parliamentary Representation of the City of Coventry, Coventry, 1888.

AUTHOR BIOGRAPHY

David McGrory's family came to Coventry in 1882 when his great grandfather was based in the local barracks. He married a local girl and David's father and grandfather were both born opposite Bablake, within the old city wall. David is Coventry's best-known historian, who has made both television and radio appearances, he also writes the popular Time Tunnel series in the Coventry Evening Telegraph. David has also written more books on the city than any other historian before him.

Francis Frith
Pioneer Victorian Photographer

Francis Frith, founder of the world-famous photographic archive, was a multi-talented man. A devout Quaker and a highly successful Victorian businessman, he was philosophical by nature and pioneering in outlook. By 1855 he had already established a wholesale grocery business in Liverpool, and sold it for the astonishing sum of £200,000, which is the equivalent today of over £15,000,000. Now in his thirties, and captivated by the new science of photography, Frith set out on a series of pioneering journeys up the Nile and to the Near East.

He was the first photographer to venture beyond the sixth cataract of the Nile. Africa was still the mysterious 'Dark Continent', and Stanley and Livingstone's historic meeting was a decade into the future. The conditions for picture taking confound belief. He laboured for hours in his wicker dark-room in the sweltering heat of the desert, while the volatile chemicals fizzed dangerously in their trays. Back in London he exhibited his photographs and was 'rapturously cheered' by members of the Royal Society. His reputation as a photographer was made overnight.

By the 1870s the railways had threaded their way across the country, and Bank Holidays and half-day Saturdays had been made obligatory by Act of Parliament. All of a sudden the working man and his family were able to enjoy days out, take holidays, and see a little more of the world.

With typical business acumen, Francis Frith foresaw that these new tourists would enjoy having souvenirs to commemorate their days out. For the next thirty years he travelled the country by train and by pony and trap, producing fine photographs of seaside resorts and beauty spots that were keenly bought by millions of Victorians. These prints were painstakingly pasted into family albums and pored over during the dark nights of winter, rekindling precious memories of summer excursions. Frith's studio was soon supplying retail shops all over the country, and by 1890 F Frith & Co had become the greatest specialist photographic publishing company in the world, with over 2,000 sales outlets, and pioneered the picture postcard.

Francis Frith had died in 1898 at his villa in Cannes, his great project still growing. By 1970 the archive he created contained over a third of a million pictures showing 7,000 British towns and villages.

Frith's legacy to us today is of immense significance and value, for the magnificent archive of evocative photographs he created provides a unique record of change in the cities, towns and villages throughout Britain over a century and more. Frith and his fellow studio photographers revisited locations many times down the years to update their views, compiling for us an enthralling and colourful pageant of British life and character.

We are fortunate that Frith was dedicated to recording the minutiae of everyday life. For it is this sheer wealth of visual data, the painstaking chronicle of changes in dress, transport, street layouts, buildings, housing and landscape that captivates us so much today, offering us a powerful link with the past and with the lives of our ancestors.

Computers have now made it possible for Frith's many thousands of images to be accessed almost instantly. The archive offers every one of us an opportunity to examine the places where we and our families have lived and worked down the years. Its images, depicting our shared past, are now bringing pleasure and enlightenment to millions around the world a century and more after his death. For further information visit: **www.francisfrith.com**

FRITH PRODUCTS & SERVICES

Francis Frith would doubtless be pleased to know that the pioneering publishing venture he started in 1860 still continues today. Over a hundred and forty years later, The Francis Frith Collection continues in the same innovative tradition and is now one of the foremost publishers of vintage photographs in the world. Some of the current activities include:

INTERIOR DECORATION

Today Frith's photographs can be seen framed and as giant wall murals in thousands of pubs, restaurants, hotels, banks, retail stores and other public buildings throughout the country. In every case they enhance the unique local atmosphere of the places they depict and provide reminders of gentler days in an increasingly busy and frenetic world.

PRODUCT PROMOTIONS

Frith products are used by many major companies to promote the sales of their own products or to reinforce their own history and heritage. Frith promotions have been used by Hovis bread, Courage beers, Scots Porage Oats, Colman's mustard, Cadbury's foods, Mellow Birds coffee, Dunhill pipe tobacco, Guinness, and Bulmer's Cider.

GENEALOGY AND FAMILY HISTORY

As the interest in family history and roots grows world-wide, more and more people are turning to Frith's photographs of Great Britain for images of the towns, villages and streets where their ancestors lived; and, of course, photographs of the churches and chapels where their ancestors were christened, married and buried are an essential part of every genealogy tree and family album.

FRITH PRODUCTS

All Frith photographs are available Framed or just as Mounted Prints and unmounted versions. These may be ordered from the address below. Other products available are - Calendars, Jigsaws, Canvas Prints, Mugs, Tea Towels, Tableware and local and prestige books.

THE INTERNET

Over several hundred thousand Frith photographs can be viewed and purchased on the internet through the Frith websites!

For more detailed information on Frith products, look at www.francisfrith.com

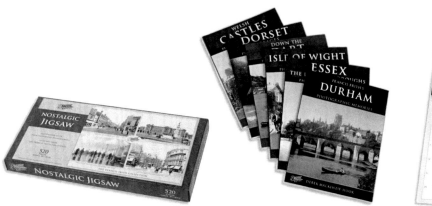

See the complete list of Frith Books at: www.francisfrith.com
This web site is regularly updated with the latest list of publications from The Francis Frith Collection. If you wish to buy books relating to another part of the country that your local bookshop does not stock, you may purchase on-line.

For further information, trade, or author enquiries please contact us at the address below:
The Francis Frith Collection, 19 Kingsmead Business Park, Gillingham, Dorset SP8 5FB.
Tel: +44 (0)1722 716 376   Email: sales@francisfrith.co.uk

See Frith products on the internet at www.francisfrith.com

FREE PRINT OF YOUR CHOICE
CHOOSE A PHOTOGRAPH FROM THIS BOOK
+ POSTAGE

Mounted Print
Overall size 14 x 11 inches (355 x 280mm)

TO RECEIVE YOUR FREE PRINT

Choose any Frith photograph in this book

Simply complete the Voucher opposite and return it with your payment (to cover postage and handling) and we will print the photograph of your choice in SEPIA (size 11 x 8 inches) and supply it in a cream mount ready to frame (overall size 14 x 11 inches).

Order additional Mounted Prints at HALF PRICE - £19.00 each (normally £38.00)

If you would like to order more Frith prints from this book, possibly as gifts for friends and family, you can buy them at half price (with no additional postage costs).

Have your Mounted Prints framed

For an extra £20.00 per print you can have your mounted print(s) framed in an elegant polished wood and gilt moulding, overall size 16 x 13 inches (no additional postage required).

IMPORTANT!

❶ Please note: aerial photographs and photographs with a reference number starting with a "Z" are not Frith photographs and cannot be supplied under this offer.

❷ Offer valid for delivery to one UK address only.

❸ These special prices are only available if you use this form to order. You must use the ORIGINAL VOUCHER on this page (no copies permitted). We can only despatch to one UK address.

❹ This offer cannot be combined with any other offer.

As a customer your name & address will be stored by Frith but not sold or rented to third parties. Your data will be used for the purpose of this promotion only.

Send completed Voucher form to:
**The Francis Frith Collection,
1 Chilmark Estate House, Chilmark,
Salisbury, Wiltshire SP3 5DU**

Voucher for FREE and Reduced Price Frith Prints

Please do not photocopy this voucher. Only the original is valid, so please fill it in, cut it out and return it to us with your order.

Picture ref no	Page no	Qty	Mounted @ £19.00	Framed + £20.00	Total Cost £
		1	Free of charge*	£	£
			£19.00	£	£
			£19.00	£	£
			£19.00	£	£
			£19.00	£	£
			£19.00	£	£

Please allow 28 days for delivery. Offer available to one UK address only

	* Post & handling	£3.80
	Total Order Cost	£

Title of this book ....

I enclose a cheque/postal order for £ ....
made payable to 'The Francis Frith Collection'

OR please debit my Mastercard / Visa / Maestro card, details below

Card Number:

Issue No (Maestro only):   Valid from (Maestro):

Card Security Number: Expires:

Signature:

Name Mr/Mrs/Ms ....

Address ....

....

....

.... Postcode ....

Daytime Tel No ....

Email ....

Valid to 31/12/24

Free Print – see overleaf

Can you help us with information about any of the Frith photographs in this book?

We are gradually compiling an historical record for each of the photographs in the Frith archive. It is always fascinating to find out the names of the people shown in the pictures, as well as insights into the shops, buildings and other features depicted.

If you recognize anyone in the photographs in this book, or if you have information not already included in the author's caption, do let us know. We would love to hear from you, and will try to publish it in future books or articles.

An Invitation from The Francis Frith Collection to Share Your Memories

The 'Share Your Memories' feature of our website allows members of the public to add personal memories relating to the places featured in our photographs, or comment on others already added. Seeing a place from your past can rekindle forgotten or long held memories. Why not visit the website, find photographs of places you know well and add YOUR story for others to read and enjoy? We would love to hear from you!

www.francisfrith.com/memories

Our production team

Frith books are produced by a small dedicated team at offices near Salisbury. Most have worked with the Frith Collection for many years. All have in common one quality: they have a passion for the Frith Collection.

Frith Books and Gifts

We have a wide range of books and gifts available on our website utilising our photographic archive, many of which can be individually personalised.

www.francisfrith.com

Contains material sourced from responsibly managed forests.